SEATTLE

NOW & THEN
volume 2

This is the NOW to the front cover's THEN. Depressing isn't it? Or is it? You may, perhaps, enjoy the convenience of a fast car and a Big Mac to the comfort of a canoe on a slow river and a wicker basket filled with a home-prepared lunch. But, of course, here the choice—of the transport, not the lunch— is no longer ours. The Black River is lost. But before it was deliberately drained it ran right through these parking lots on its serpentine way from Lake Washington to Elliott Bay. This book is a collection of 86 such NOW-&-THENs. Most of them are taken from within the Seattle city limits, but others like this Renton scene are drawn from the surrounding region. In this collection you can start anywhere, so you may wish to start with story #38 which is of the Black River and so also of the Big Mac.

ISBN 0-9614357-2-0

Bill Burden

Introduction

I should, perhaps, simply leap across the introduction and go straight to the acknowledgments. And I should start with the photographers who have been photographing this city now for 127 years. In many of these 86 stories they are named, but usually not.

Acknowledgements

ca. 1901

Peiser
SECOND St. No. ?
SEATTLE

THEO. E.
Peiser

INSTANTANEOUS ∗ PHOTOGRAPHER,

NO. 817 SECOND STREET, NEAR MARION,

SEATTLE, W. T.

Often we simply do not know *who* they were, while still being thankful *that they were.* So then after the traditionally neglected photographers who is next for these acknowledgments? I choose Jim Faber, who while I sit here a little queasy with a deadline stomach, is enjoying slices of London Broil au Nihon (which a vegetarian like myself discovers is a entree of thinly-sliced roast beef) and strawberries dipped in chocolate and doused with Grande Marnier at the 38th Annual Old Timers Banquet of the Puget Sound Maritime Historical Society. Perhaps about now Jim is addressing the group beneath the dome in the Dome Room of the Arctic Club on the "Return of the Mosquito Fleet." Both the speaker and the subject are a surprise—by now a pleasant one I hope. For the program lists me as the "evening's addressee". But I have been injured and am at this moment, only good for writing acknowledgements. So, obviously, I start with Jim Faber.

Jim, did not exactly come off the bench to do this filling in. The author of *Steamer's Wake,* which is—without any argument—the best history of Northwest steamboating ever assembled (the word "assembled" is not really organic enough for Faber's heartfelt work), is also the best possible speaker the PSMHS could have asked for. The reason they did not is because the two of them, Faber and the Society, had been extraordinarily thick with one another throughout the last year. First, the PSMHS has now on exhibit in their wing at the Museum of History and Industry an

exhibit based on Jim's book. So in this photo we see Faber somewhat candidly inspecting one of the photos in the exhibit with PSMHS activist Loretta Valentine. The exhibit, as of this writing, is still up so go see it! I did, of course, and more. I took two of Jim's photos and used them here in this my second volume of "now-&-thens." (You'll find them in stories 33 and 68, and in the latter feature you will discover yet another picture of Jim again

moment so are the serenely stuffed beef-and-chocolate eaters of our Puget Sound Maritime Historical Society. Although they heard from you not six months before, they have, no doubt, enjoyed (you have I imagine by now concluded your talk) traveling yet again on that Northwest natural resource your pioneer parents named Jim.

And now for the rest of you. But what are the mechanics for acknowledging everyone? You make a list and then check it off. But when you are done you are, damn-it-all, not done. You will have forgotten someone and they will stay so until after the printers have made your unconscious neglect indelible. So you now-forgotten-ones, forgive me. And you too, dear reader, please forgive me for all those other mistakes I've made below that will sometimes make reading my text like walking barefoot across a farmer's driveway. But the truth is I care about typos and other such pesky casualties of illiteracy only so much. And neither will I accept all of the responsibility. If those I acknowledge below get some of the credit, surely, they should also take some of the blame. So in one broad gesture I thank and admonish them.

somewhat candidly running his authoritative finger across the same photo with PSMHS member and tonight, diseased shirker, Paul Dorpat. Faber is wearing his nautical shirt at the gala opening of his and the Society's exhibit. The photographer was MOHAI's Howard Giske, another old friend, whose help also I must here acknowledge— although it was my camera.)

Before we leave Jim Faber to finish his speech before the society and after the strawberries dipped in chocolate, let's return to his book (do you have your copy?) remembering his subject, "The Return of the Mosquito Fleet." There, in the last paragraph of the forward to Faber's book, Murray Morgan pays a tribute to the faith of his old friend, Jim Faber. This will also do well to express my thanks. Murray writes: *"The age of steam is a memory clouded by heavier vapors. Those who never knew it may not miss it. But for those who remember, like Jim Faber, there is the dream, the faith, that some new technology will bring back the day when the most travelled highway is one that ebbs and flows and ever enriches those it carries."*

So thanks for carrying me, Jim Faber. I am enriched, and I feel confident that at this very

Begin with this photo. (I mean, of course, those in it. I share with other photo-historians the trance-like foible of objectifying the photo itself as the subject.) This is the core of the lay-out crew. Therefore, these are the professionals who are guilty for whatever imprudent use of white space might crop-up (or down) below. Here, right to left, *front row* Jean Emmons, Sam Garriot, *back row* Nina Curell, Bill Burden and *in appropriate T-shirt* the longest-sitting member of the Bumbershoot Advisory Committee. All have stepped out from the details of lay-out to sit

Courtesy of Michael Maslan

(Actually, we never got around to putting page numbers on Volume One. This I now regret... for reasons of scholarly reference all books which might be useful to researchers should have them.)

As with the first volume so with this Genny McCoy did a summer's worth of editing and typing the hardcopy (on paper) of my stories onto the computer's disk. And this time it was not a floppy. It was hard, because David Halliday (who can usually be found pouring over science fiction at the Allegro coffee house) of *MICROFT SYSTEMS* trained my Korean IBM-compatible to remember all the now-&-then books I could ever produce in a long life of productive nows reflecting on their thens.

There are two others I should thankfully acknowledge within this context of computers—the one has never used one and the other needs to get away from them. The former, my oldest brother Ted, is a local psychoanalyst who writes all his articles and books long-hand. (But, then, so did Freud.) Yet he knows a good deal on a data-processor when he sees one, and helped put beneath me the keyboard I am now punching. So having an older brother who's a psychiatrist can have its consoling moments, and here he is propping me up for yet another unidentified photographer, with brothers Dave and Norm behind. (This then is also the book's conventional photograph of the author—with but then a babbling biography.)

down in the autumnal sun on a Wallingford porch and tackle instead the flip side of Atlas' work and balance a french comedian on top of the world while posing for this photograph.

Something more should be said about all of them, but won't be—except for Jean who turned her eye for subtle coloring upon our covers and hand-painted both the Black River scene and the pioneer waterfront scene.

Paula Calderon and Genevieve McCoy should be with this group but are not because they were doing something more important—the former studying mind-control and the latter intellectual history for her third Ph.D. exam. Paula did the indexing for this *VOLUME TWO* of my Now-&-Then features and tricked the computer into believing that all 86 stories collected here were only one page long. So the index listing is done to stories not pages. Why?, you may ask. Because the pagination of these self-published SEATTLE NOW & THEN volumes is the very last thing done.

Steve Herold of *LASERGRAPHICS* is Volume Two's second computer interface. Steve's an old friend who has a profound sympathy for typefaces. Every hair on his head ends in a serif. I met Steve first in those fecund 60's when he was a bookstore owner with an education in calligraphy from Reed College. Steve filled the windows of his ID Bookstore, a 60's University District landmark, with the etchings of William Blake—and also with pages from the Kamasutra Calendar of ancient Hindu "centerfolds". For that he was busted for what must have been the most comic harassment of those often wonderfully surreal years. Now Steve is manipulating the versatile icons of a MacIntosh pagemaker and thereby arranged this text into its—easy for him—relatively conventional shapes.

When Steve home-delivered the last of Volume Two's typeset copy (excepting this introduction) he spied one of the books in my London collection, opened it to a page on Greenwich and murmured, "Hmmm I used to live near there." "When?", I asked. "In the 60s—early 60s." "And what were you doing in London in the early 60s?", I responded. "Walking about, and studying in the British Museum." "And what were you studying?" "This and that." Silenced by Steve's London shadow, I stupidly forgot to ask him what he'd been studying precisely in the famous reading room of the British Museum, but will when I deliver this introduction to LaserGraphics. Actually, Bill Burden—pictured above—will deliver it. My old and close friend Bill has to be plugged into this computer set as well. Many a time he has rescued me from my electronic passivity with his binary confidence. Bill has also helped update a number of the "now" photographs in this volume. Beneath those you will see that he is one photographer who *is* credited.

Genny McCoy is the other one. I am responsible for all the rest of them—the so-called "now" photos which in this modern American megatropolis are quickly slipping into the "then". I should add that when McCoy was at the computer she also had a free-hand at recasting my frequent illiteracies into her own sensible style. Therefore, she too may be blamed for whatever bombs can and do drop from my prose.

Now for the "then". The historical photos come from 12 years of more than full-time searching for them. After the photographers, those who get the credit are the people who carefully take care of the photographs and especially those who realize that an important part of this caring is sharing. My first mentors in this humane regard were Robert Monroe and Dennis Andersen, now long gone from the Historical Photography Collection at the University of Washington. But there are others who continue to keep and organize these treasures in the city's several public archives, including, besides the University, the Museum of History and Industry (MOHAI) and the Seattle Public Library. Some of their names are, Susan Cunningham, Glenda Pearson, Carla Rickerson, Richard Engeman, Bill Dahl, Mike Cerelli and Rod Slemmons. I thank them all.

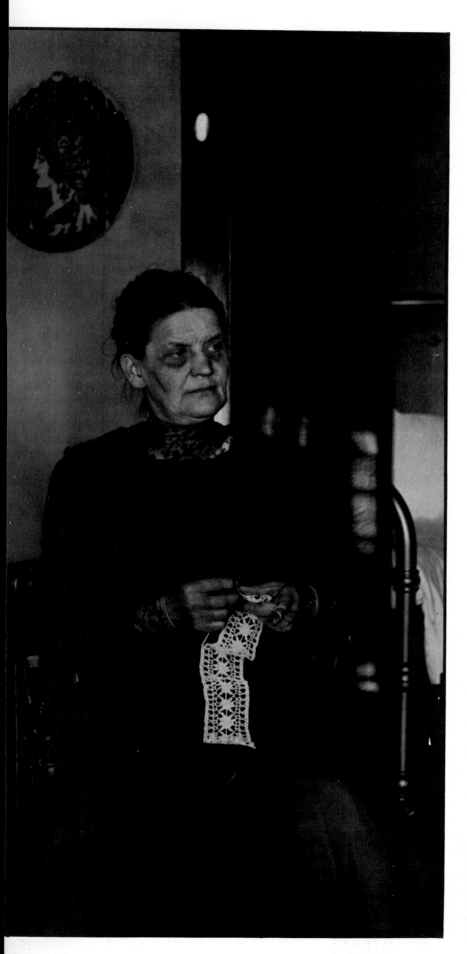

I cannot begin to acknowledge all of the individual collectors who have helped me by generously sharing with me—and so you—their discoveries and cherished collections. For some of them it's a week-end habit of searching through garage sales; for others it's an insomniac obsession that might be compared to an uncontrollable appetite for a controlled substance, except that they all seem unusually happy and healthy. I want especially to thank John and Lael Hanawalt of the Old Seattle Paperworks in the Pike Place Market, Michael Maslan (who is both truly impassioned with the search and generous), William Mix, Taylor Bowie, Lucy Campbell Coe, Warren Wing, Greg Lane, Bill Greer, Don Myer, and Lawton and Jean Gowey.

Others who have helped in some way with the production of Volume Two are Stan Smith of *Argentum* who wrestled with the colors on the cover, Susan Starfield of *Goodtime Harbor Tours* who arranged for Bill Burden to photograph the needed off-shore shots of the city, Vito Perillo of *Pacific Pipeline* who is helping with the book's distribution, and the sisters Fury—Kaylin and Carson—who sacrificed several summer weekend hours to help dry and wax the screened prints.

As with the first volume I should also thank here an old college friend, Dick Moultrie who originally got me interested in local history when he asked for my help in researching the past of Pioneer Square's Merchants Cafe. And I also again thank Michael Wiater for urging me to stick with it. This is also a proper context in which to again thank Ed and Carolyn Littlefield for making my years of research and publishing often substantially easier with their generous assistance. Volume One was dedicated, in part, to them.

For nearly five years now I've been writing my "Now-&-Then" feature for *The Seattle Times*, and this volume like the first one is taken, in part, from that Pacific Magazine feature. "In part", because the articles as they appear here are always longer and include more photographs than the newspaper stories. I want to thank the Pacific's editor Kathy Andrisevic for both her continued confidence in the column and her good humor. Ginny Merdes, and sometimes Tom Stockley read the copy I submit and are generally gentle. And I want to remember again that it was Erik Lacitis' advocacy that guided me into the inner-sanctums of *The Times*.

There are many others to acknowledge including, perhaps, even Ronald Reagan. Choosing a printer for *SEATTLE NOW & THEN, Volume One* was the most difficult eleventh-hour decision I had to make. The comparison of the bids and services between Craftsman Press and what was then still called Grange Printers was so close that I was simply stuck in choosing between them.

When I at last had but hours left to decide I made my way, first, nervously to Grange Press for some final questions. On my way down Fairview Ave. just beyond the City Light steam plant at the SW corn-er of Lake Union, I was mysteriously inhibited by a traffic jam backed up all the way to St. Vincent De Paul. It was an extraordinary mess for a week-day afternoon, but my old and familiar escape was open to me down the dirt track between the street and the waterfront. So in a rush with my dilemma I turned onto the old shortcut and was soon sur-rounded by business suits with unusually big men that looked curiously alike poured into them. They persuaded me to exit not the scene but my car, and explain what I was doing in the middle of Reagan's route to the Seattle Center (and, as I later learned, Husky coach Don James' first and last political speech.)

The sweat on the back of my neck was the warmest response I've had in years to national pol-itics. I hurriedly and fancifully explained to the

men in suits that I was on my way to the *Wawona*, the sailing ship that floats beside the Center for Wooden Boats at the south end of the lake. And in that moment as I lied to the Secret Service I looked up at Craftsman Press, (in the old Ford Assembly plant across Fairview), and made my decision—or rather Ronald Reagan made it for me. And so while I missed his speech, did not vote with his landslide (remember, I live in Walling-ford), and did not make it to Grange Press, still I thank him for the leadership that extracted me, although not without some sweat, from my dilemma.

The decision was a good one—Craftsman did a fine job and did it on time. But this is a new book, a new bid, and this time I made it all the way to Grange Press, since renamed Valco, asked my questions and stayed. So while I thank Bob Dennis for all his help with Volume One, now I thank Mel Carlson and Bob Valentine for theirs, with an encouragement that we get this thing out on time.

You see, dear reader, you are to blame for this anxiety over scheduling. You buy 99 percent of your books just before Christmas, which means: 1. that you probably will not read them yourself, and 2. that we, the authors, don't know if those to whom you give them will read them either. So after all the rushing is done I'm left with the awkward anxiety that perhaps I was just running for the coffee table. However, *you dear reader* have gotten this far and for that I thank you. Now please do continue for the conclusion.

A postscript to this story is that I did make it to the *Wawona*, and sincerely so. That story, number 15, is included here. And as this photo should prove, I did not go directly to Craftsman Press the day I got stuck with Ronald Reagan but waited for him to zoom off the Mercer St. I-5 exit and shoot past me while I captured him—photographically—in his very awesome limousine. In my portrait of the President you can, I believe, make out his primary features— the kind of essential shape of the man that Konrad Lorenz taught us baby ducks recognize in their parents. However, one thing you cannot discover from the portrait (and I am quite confident in this) is that Ronald Reagan did wave to me—and the agents around me.

The man on the left is watching me—not the President whose limo is just turning the corner in front of the Craftsman Press Plant.

The blurred but familiar face of the President.

Thanks also to Susan Gerard, Dan Patterson, Shiela Farr, Ann Faber, Celeste Franklin, Marjorie Steinbrueck for permission to use Victor Steinbrueck's sketch of the old Kalmar Hotel (see story #27); Kay Bullitt whose energy and civic sense are guided by goodwill (I agree with her inspiration that there is still time to change our city's nickname from the rather brittle "Emerald" to the "Goodwill City". Such a name would be really *created and recreated.* What you do with an emerald is merely look at it, wear it, or sell it.) And thanks to Rosa and Murray Morgan. I dedicated Volume One, in part, to Murray. Here in Volume Two he puts an end to the last story's last line as I follow him into the wilds of Puget Sound.

Now Jim Faber has returned from the Old Timers Banquet and calls to tell me that the rare roast beef was delicious, the vegetables fresh, the new potatoes browned in butter, and his speech well received. And from the evening's program he reads to me the last line—the Puget Sound Maritime Historical Society's description of their *"ADDRESS OF EVENING by Historian, Author and Photographer par excellence, Paul Dorpat."* Jim assures me that I was very well received, and that several persons say I was never better.

I, if you could not yet tell, dedicate this book to Jim Faber.

Rosa and Murray Morgan at Wilson Point.

Ronald McDonald as seen through the window of the Renton McDonalds.

Jim Faber adjusts his hat.

Table of Contents

Courtesy of Michael Maslan

1   The Sidewheeler *Alida*

The scene above is the second oldest surviving photographic record of Seattle's waterfront. The view was made from the end of Henry Yesler's wharf, and looks across his mill pond to the sidewheeler *Alida*.

Above and behind the steamship's paddle is the dirt intersection of Marion St. and Front St. (now First Ave). That puts the *Alida* in the parking lot now bordered by Post and Western avenues and Columbia and Marion streets—or just behind the Colman Building.

The occasion is either in the summer of 1870 or 1871. The steeple-topped Methodist Protestant Church on the left was built in 1864, as we see it here. In the summer of 1872 its builder and pastor, Rev. Daniel Bagley, added a second story with a mansard roof. Bagley was also the main force behind the construction of the University of Washington, the classic white structure with the dome-shaped cupola at the center horizon.

The photograph's third tower, on the right, tops Seattle's first public school. Central School was built in 1870 back

William Fife's 1872 rendering of Seattle from Elliott Bay includes some of the same landmarks showing in the photographs on these pages and those following.

Courtesy of Old Seattle Paperworks, Pike Place Market

away from the northwest corner of Third and Madison. If the bell in its belltower were still calling classes, it would be clanging near the main banking lobby of the Seafirst tower.

The *Alida*'s 115-foot keel was laid in Olympia in 1869, but its upper structure was completed in Seattle, in June of the following year, at Hammond's boat yard near the foot of Columbia St.—or just to the right of this scene. Perhaps, the occasion for this photograph is shortly after her inaugural launching.

The *Alida* first tested the water on June 29, 1870. Captain E. A. Starr invited Seattle's establishment on the roundtrip trial run to Port Townsend. The July 4 edition of the *Weekly Intelligencer* reported that "During the passage down, the beautiful weather, the delightful scenery, the rapid and easy progress

made, and last though not least, the excellent instrumental and vocal music which was furnished by the ladies, all contributed to the enjoyment of the occasion." The steam to Port Townsend took four hours and eight minutes, and a little more on the return.

The *Alida*'s 20-year career on Puget Sound began with a few months of glory. She was the first steamship to successfully intrude on the monopoly which another sidewheeler, the *Eliza Anderson*, had on the Sound. The *Alida*'s owners, the Starr brothers, had won from the Alida's triumph, however, was shortlived. She was too slow and too light for the open waters of the straits. In 1871 the Starr brothers introduced a second and stronger sidewheeler, the *North Pacific*. For ten years it controlled the Victoria run, while the *Alida* was restricted to

steaming between Olympia and Port Townsend and way points, including Seattle.

The *Alida* came to her somewhat bizarre end in 1890. While anchored just offshore in Gig Harbor, a brush fire swept down to her mooring and burned her to the water.

A year earlier the Seattle waterfront was also swept by fire. When it was rebuilt after the Great Fire of 1889, all of what is water in this historical scene was planked over and eventually filled in to the sea wall we see in this contemporary scene, 500 feet out from First Ave.

The accompanying historical photo is considered the oldest surviving photographic record of the waterfront. Its usually dating of between 1866 and 1868 is probably about right. The printing of it on the back cover is hand-colored.

A hand-colored version of this scene appears on the book's back cover.

Courtesy of Lawton Gowey

2 Pipers on Front Street

The captioned subject of this Peterson brothers photograph is its vacant street. The brothers have inscribed "Front St. Seattle W. T. [Washington Territory]" along its dirty diagonal line.

As the scene shows, the street's name was appropriate. The Petersons took this shot in 1878 or 1879. Then, at high tide, Elliott Bay beat against the timber retaining wall that held Front St. high and dry above the waterfront. This is Seattle's first major public works—the regrading of Front St. from a stump-strewn, ravine-ridden path to a filled-in, smoothed-out highway, with guardrail and a sidewalk promenade along the city's front. The Petersons are showing it off.

The scene was shot from the balcony above Maddock's drugstore at the N.E. corner of Front's intersection with Madison St. The drugstore did not

survive the Great Fire of 1889. I took the "now" shot from the second floor of a brick building which was raised there soon after the fire, and which, in 1986, was still after half-a-century the home of Warshall's Sporting Goods.

The '89 fire started across Front St. in the Pontius Building. The corner of its balcony is on the older photo's far right. It and the Woodward Grain House, the building that dominates the photo's center, were both built on pilings. In between them is a glimpse of a section of Yesler's wharf and mill.

The Woodward was the business home of Peter's Furs, Cigars and Liquors. Peter was in the right line. The 1878 city directory claimed that "five out of every six men in the territory use tobacco, and nine out of every ten men use intoxicating drinks." However, another of the directory's statistics suggests that these prevalent vices were still lonely ones, for "There are three bachelors to every bacheloress in the territory."

Posing in the photograph's lower left-hand corner are A. W. Piper, his son Wallis, and their dog Jack. As the proprietor of the Puget Sound Candy Manufactory, Piper was very popular. The 1878 directory reviewed his co-fections as "warranted strictly pure." Both Piper's confectionary and the Peterson's studio were on Front St. near Cherry. They were, no doubt, friends.

For 30 years the Pipers lived in Seattle making candy and friends. When Piper died here in 1904, his *Post Intelligencer* obituary was an unusually good-natured one. There historian Thomas Prosch first of all remembered "Piper's cream cakes. During the 1870s they were particularly noted. The people of those days to this time think nothing of the kind...has ever approached them in excellence."

Piper was also an artist. Prosch recounted, "He could draw true to life, could mold in clay, cut stone...his Christmas display was noted for its originality, humor and beauty."

In many ways the candy-maker was unconventional. A religious Unitarian, he was also a socialist member of the Seattle City Council, and an unsuccessful Populist candidate for mayor. He was, however, a successful practical joker. Once, at a public dance, he mimicked Henry Yesler so convincingly that the real Yesler ran home to construct a sign which read "This is the only original Yesler."

Prosch concluded, "Everybody regarded him as a friend." A.W. Piper died at the age of 76, survived by Mrs. Piper, their nine children and many friends.

If you take the care to compare this 1878 scene from the end of Yesler's wharf with those in the preceeding story, you will not only detect a number of surviving landmarks, but will also see the dramatic effects the 1876 regrade of Front Street (First Ave.) had on the waterfront.

Courtesy of University of Washington Historical Photography Collection

3 The Elephant on Front Street

In this 1878 view up Front St. (now First Ave.) only the Elephant store on the right—where, presumably, both the bargains and the selections are big—is obviously a retail house. The others look like homes, but the street's residential character is slightly deceptive. One of those clapboards is a foundry; another, a cigar store; another, a drugstore; and the roof on the lower left-hand corner tops a brewery.

The Elephant Store is at Front St.'s southeast corner with Columbia, and Moses Maddock's drugstore is the dominant white structure just left of the photo's center, two blocks north at Madison St. Beyond that, Front St. was sided by homes. The many gabled Amos Brown home at Spring St. (just above the drugstore and right of the tall fir) and the Arthur Denny home at Union St. (just left of the fir) are Seattle's first grand homes. For Denny, one of the city's founders, it was his third residence when he moved there in 1865. He lived in this fancy Victorian mansion with the jigsaw trim until 1899, the year of his death. By then the house was surrounded by multi-storied hotels and department stores.

Beyond the Denny home we can see how Front St. jogs a little to the right and east, at Pike St. Pike was the northern end of the street's 1876 improvement. Before that regrading, there was a hump at Cherry St. (the site of the photographer's perch), another rise at Marion (see Story One), and a ravine at Seneca deep enough to require a bridge.

Finally this scene includes a subject, bigger than either the street or an elephant. It is the hill on the horizon—Denny Hill. Here the top of it reaches about 100 ft. above the present elevation of Third Ave. between Stewart and Virginia streets. This is the best early record of Denny Hill that survives, while the hill itself, of course, did not.

This rare view up Front St. looks from the top of the Occidental Hotel (see story #7) about 1885. The mansard roof of the Frye Opera House is on the right.

Front St., again north of Cherry, under the blanket of the 1880 Snow.

The ravages of the Great Fire of 1889 on Front St. looking here north from Cherry St. Somewhere in there are the ashes of the Elephant Store.

Like the Elephant and the Snow this scene looks north from the foot of Cherry. Here the date is α 1905, about 27 years after the elephant!

4 Henry Villard's Grand Occasion

On September 14, 1883 Northern Pacific Railroad president Henry Villard and his entourage of governors, senators, and railroaders came into town not by rail but aboard the steamship *Queen of the Pacific*. Seattle was ready.

Pioneer historian Thomas Prosch was also ready and waiting and later wrote, "Seattle citizens made extraordinary preparations for the reception, never before or since equaled in the town on any occasion. The streets had been thoroughly cleaned and adorned for miles with evergreen trees, arches [like the one in this historical scene] bunting and appropriate emblems and sentiments...It was a fine day."

One week earlier, on September 8, the east and west ends of the nation's second transcontinental railroad joined in Montana with a golden spike driven by Henry Villard himself. And in the days that followed "every considerable place" along the new line, including Portland and Tacoma, erected arches and marched the Villard party beneath them.

The Villard arch in the historical photograph straddled Commercial St. (now First Ave. S.) at Mill St. (now Yesler Way). It was constructed on the enthused faith that Villard would soon bring his promised railroad into the Queen City as well. Then the Northern Pacific only reached as far as the "City of Destiny," as Tacoma called itself. But although Villard passed beneath his Seattle arch, his railroad did not soon pass into town. Henry Villard shortly lost control of the Northern Pacific to powers who favored the railroad's chosen Puget Sound terminus, Tacoma. And Seattle had to angrily wait years more for what it was joyfully anticipating on September 14, 1883.

Left The Territorial University, at 4th and Seneca decked out for the Villard company ceremonies.

When it was built in the mid 1870s the Arlington House was the largest building in Washington Territory. Here its decorated with its own now-&-then banners for Villard's pleasure. Destroyed in the 1889 Fire, the Globe bldg replaced it, (lower-left) now the home of the Elliott Bay Bookstore at First S. and Main St.

Courtesy of Lawton Gowey

5 First Avenue South from King Street

Genevieve McCoy

Photographers are opportunists, and sometime (probably) in 1903 one grabbed the chance to climb high above the center of First Ave. S., point a lens north and shoot this historical scene. On what temporary perch that photographer steadied his or her bulky camera, we may never know, but the view looking north from King St. is wonderfully revealing.

We will start at the bottom. The tracks that cut diagonally across the scene are part of the main railroad line through town. The Great Northern did not begin cutting its tunnel beneath the city until May of 1903, and it took two years more to complete it. That tunnel was bored to ease the congestion of boxcars on the waterfront and the frequent interruptions of traffic here on First Ave. S.

The year 1903 is a good guess for dating this scene. Here's the evidence. In the hole on the right at the southeast corner of First S. and Jackson St., foundation work is beginning on a building which was completed in 1904.

Now it's called the Heritage Building after the Heritage Group that recently renovated it. However, we remember it best as the recent home of Standard Brands and before that of Wax & Rain, another paint supplier.

Beyond the pit is another clue for this date-of-choice, the electric trolley on Jackson St. Although its markings are too small to decipher in this printing, a magnified inspection of the original photo reveals the number "324" on the trolley's side. Car 324 was built in St. Louis in 1902 for the Seattle Electric Co., but was soon sold to the Puget Sound Electric Railway for service on its then new Seattle Tacoma Interurban line. Here, enroute to Tacoma, it will turn off Jackson onto First S. and soon pass on the tracks, right of center, just beneath the photographer's perch.

Behind Car 324 is the Capitol Brewing Co. building. Built in 1900 it was the Seattle office for Olympia Beer and home of the Tumwater Tavern. The familiar brewery symbol of the horse-shoe-framed waterfall is stuck to the stone just left of the trolley.

This pleasing three-story combination of brick and stone is still standing and renamed the Jackson Building. The old Olympia sign is gone and in its place there should be (but isn't) a plaque telling how the architect Ralph Anderson boldly bought this modest neoclassical structure in 1963 and, with help from a lot of preservationist friends, began the fight to save this entire neighborhood. Bill Speidel soon joined him with the above ground offices for his Underground Tours, and Richard White, who now owns the building, opened his first gallery here.

Their long battle was largely won with the institution of the Pioneer Square Historical District. But the fight continues. A recent victory is on the photo's left. Just across First Ave. S. from the Jackson Building, the elegant Smith Building was also built in 1900. For half a century it was the home of Steinberg Clothing. In 1982 it was lavishly renovated into 24 large loft studio apartments where photographers and graphic designers have enough undivided room beneath 16-ft. ceilings to both live and work.

In 1903 there were so few motorcars around that if one sputtered by, you would run out to see it. In this scene, aside from the trolleys, everything is still, to quote the contemporary master saddlemaker Jack Duncan, "Horse, Horse and Horse."

That's Jack Duncan at the bottom of the "now" photograph and above him is Seattle's last horse. Jack Duncan helped me out. I was not so lucky as the historical photographer to find a temporary platform above the center of First S. at King St., and so I moved one block south for Duncan's horse, hospitality, and loan of a ladder. There I took the contemporary shot leaning against the family business that has been making "Everything For The Horse Since 1898."

The second contemporary view up First Ave. S. was photographed from the roof of the old Seattle Hardware Co. Building at the southwest corner of First and King, and is, therefore, somewhat closer to the prospect of the historical photo. The Seattle Hardware Building was recently renamed 83 King Street after a renovation that converted this distinguished warehouse into the home of a restaurant, health club, and offices in the largest Class A office renovation project in Pioneer Square.

SEATTLE.—COMMERCIAL STREET, LOOKING NORTH FROM JACKSON STREET.

Courtesy of University of Washington Historical Photography Collection

Commercial St. (First Ave. S.)—the three block commercial heart of the pre-1889-fire Seattle from Jackson St. (foreground) to Mill St. (Yesler Way) in the distance. This etching is from the mid 1880s.

6 Pioneer Mourning — Sept. 26, 1881

U nder the headline, "GOD REIGNS AND THE GOVERNMENT AT WASHINGTON STILL LIVES" the *Intelligencer* newspaper for Tuesday September 27, 1881 reported on the memorial service the previous day for the fallen president James Abram Garfield.

The lead paragraph begins, "The booming of cannon AWAKENED our people from their slumbers yesterday morning, and they rose to behold a bright and beautiful day dawning upon them." In the surviving photos of the memorial scene we can detect that the people after rising to the sun are, later in the day, hiding from it beneath bumbershoots.

The crowd has assembled in Occidental Square (now Pioneer Square) in front of the Occidental Hotel (now the site of the "Sinking Ship" parking garage) to be consoled by the mourning hymns of the Episcopal choir, solemnized by the dirges of the Pacific Cornets and edified by speakers.

Garfield's portrait is surrounded by the red-white-blue-and-black bunting above the speaker's stand. Before it, Orange Jacobs, the principal orator of the day and personal friend of Garfield, added to the day's bright light by describing the assassinated president as "The sun-intellect of this nation, reflecting the light of his noble deeds...tinging the breaking clouds of dissension with the beauty and effulgence of hope and peace." (Garfield had been in office only a few months when he was shot on July 2 by a disgruntled office-seeker. He lingered on painfully until his death on Sept. 19. Throughout the nation great public memorial services like this one followed.)

The *Intelligencer* reprinted Jacob's entire speech, and the full four columns of oratory grandiloquently concluded with the headline about "God...and the Government," which the newspaper borrowed for its headline.

Although this memorial service was, no doubt, Seattle's biggest public event to that time, it did not portend so much for the city's future as another same day event. For it was on the last Monday of September 1881 that Reginald H. Thomson came to town. Seattle's future city engineer, who would later build its water and sewer systems and regrade its hills, attended the Garfield memorial; he's probably in this picture. Thomson later remembered the "profound attention that was paid to the addresses."

Also here are Yesler Way on the right, and the tower of Trinity Episcopal church on the top left. James St. is on the left partially hidden behind Henry Yesler's maple trees. The following year, 1882, three prisoners accused of murder, were dragged from the city jail and lynched from these branches. There was no memorial service.

(To the three photographs of this event with which I've been long familiar, I can now add this fourth which is also the clearest. It was taken from an original print loaned to me by Lucy Campbell Coe who was born in Seattle only six years after the Garfield memorial service. She will reach her centennial in January, 1987.

Left An Underground Tour heads across First Ave.

7 The Winter of 1884

This snow scene of Pioneer Square is one of the jewels of local photography. Although the surviving prints are rough—marked by stain, and time—still the setting shines through.

Set above the white, the elegant figure of the Occidental Hotel (in the center) seems palatial. And in the foreground the silhouette of figures forms a tableau of people idly enjoying the rare fact of snow sticking in downtown Seattle.

For three winters I have been hoping to run this "then" with an equally wintry "now", but have given up waiting. Sticking snow here is indeed a rare event, especially downtown. (I wrote this before the big pre-Thanksgiving snow of 1985.) But what event is this?

I have never encountered a convincing caption for this photograph although it's a classic. Usually it's described as a scene from the "Big Snow of 1880," but the Occidental Hotel wasn't opened until February 1884, when the Puget Sound National Bank moved into its main floor.

Although I cannot prove it (as yet) I think that February 1884 is also the date of this scene. In fact, I think this photograph was taken on either February 19 or 20 of that year.

To so conclude I needed to find another "Big Snow," and thus went on a search through the weather reports in the old *Post-Intelligencers* for the winter of 1883-1884. They were often impressionistic.

For instance, the *P.I.* reported that for Thanksgiving night (1883) "The water on the streets ran like rivers, the mud was too deep for anyone getting in it to touch bottom." But this was a rare nastiness, and on February 2, 1884 the paper reported, "February came in as bright and cheerful as January went out. The winter promises to continue to the end as warm, dry and delightful as it has so far been."

So much for prophesy. On February 8 two inches of snow fell and "it stayed on the frozen ground and was soon furnishing fair riding for the occupants of a dozen or twenty sleighs." (There are two in our scene.)

As the chill held, the snow stayed put. Lake Union froze over and on February 14, the P.I. reported that is was still "a favorite resort for our young people of the skating fraternity."

The thaw that began on the 15th was deceptive, for three days later 18 inches of fresh wet snow fell on Seattle. It was "the greatest, with a single exception, in a quarter of a century." (That exception was the really "Big Snow of 1880." The 1880 pile was actually about three times as big, with drifts up to six feet. Indeed, it was the biggest ever.)

No big snow fell during the winter of 1884-5, and by 1886 Yesler Way (on the right) and James St. (on the left) were more built up than they are in this snow scene. So I stick with the moderately big snow of Tuesday, February 19, 1884 as the occasion of this scene.

One week later, the P.I. could report, "Yesterday was balmy and Spring-like, the sun and clouds alternating, the atmosphere being pure and the temperature delightful." Very much like the February day in 1985 when I photographed the "now" scene.

Above This etching of a larger Occidental Hotel after its 1887 addition, looks across Yesler Way. The Seattle Hotel *right* its post-fire replacement (more on that in the next story) as seen across James St.

Courtesy of University of Washington Historical Photography Collection

8   Inside the Seattle Hotel

The hotel lobby with mezzanine above.

Although devoid of humans, this example of architectural photography is hardly without human interest—far from it, as a comparison of this "now" and "then" should make obvious. Where once the softly lit curves of arched windows, long-stemmed ferns and ionic capitals conspired to encourage moments of relaxed meditation, now the oil-soiled concrete of an eye-sore inspires nothing. The reader may have already concluded that this now scene was shot within the gray hull of what is grimly called the Sinking Ship—that skid road parking garage whose nihilistic construction depresses the flatiron block where James St. and Yesler Way meet at Pioneer Square.

Where the garage sinks once stood the Seattle Hotel. Although empty of people this rare photograph of the hotel's mezzanine parlor can be imagined to reveal, through the display of its comforts, every human who ever enjoyed it.

Some of those plush chairs are probably still in town. The hotel's furnishings were auctioned off in the winter of 1961, the *Times* reported, "with buyers paying upward of $16 for old wooden chairs." The razing of the landmark hotel itself began on the forenoon of April 3 of that year. This downright sleazy work was pulled off in the name of "urban renewal."

Now it's an example of black humor to recount the developers' explanations for this demolition. While assuring the sensitive that their million-dollar garage would feature "the decor of Pioneer Square" (perhaps, they were referring to the eventual garage's crowning touch— its ludicrous arched railing), they described their project as a demonstration to "eastern capital" that Seattle has faith in the future of the lower downtown area. They "challenged" the city and other property owners to follow suit and carry out the urban renewal.

These curving pipe arches were the "Sinking Ship's" minimal answer—its developer's "challenge"—to the style of Pioneer Square. *right.*

Ultimately and happily the city responded not with renewal but with renovation. But it took a lot of pushing through those forward-looking, swept-wing days of Century 21 to create a Pioneer Square Historic District.

One of those early pushers for the human future in the architecture of the past was 12-year-old Christy Nelsen, who when she read of the announced razing of the Seattle Hotel spent 34 cents on a special delivery letter to the *Times*. It reads, in part, "Why don't you adults use your heads? The Seattle Hotel is one of our most historic buildings, and you are letting some million dollars be wasted on a gas station to be built on top of it. Most everyone who reads this paper is a citizen. Well, why don't these citizens help it now? It needs help desperately in preserving its old and historic buildings."

Courtesy of Lawton Gowey

Courtesy of Lawton Gowey

Above The Seattle Hotel has been identified by perhaps a tourist or booster in this mid-1890s postcard view of Pioneer Square up Yesler Way. This is a good scene to compare with the 1884 snow shot in the preceeding story.

The Seattle hotel in its last days, *right,* and in its last day, *above.*

Courtesy of Lawton Gowey

9 Seattle's Stolen Totem

One of the most familiar stories out of Seattle's past is of the red-handed origin of its totem pole. This week's scene of the Pioneer Square unveiling was first published in the *P.I.* of Oct. 19, 1899 on the morning after the ceremony. The report's front page oversized lead paragraph reads, in part, "Greeted by the cheers of a multitude of people and the rumble and roar of the busy streets, the Alaska totem pole was presented to the city of Seattle by the Chamber of Commerce Committee of Fifteen...at 2:30 p.m., yesterday. Emphatically unique, startling, barbaric, bizarre, the gigantic carving stands solidly near the apex of the little green triangle, each fantastical figure facing resolutely up First Ave., northwestwardly, in the direction of its ancient home...."

If the raven atop the totem could have seen as far northwest as its old Fort Tongass home it would, no doubt, have been staring at the stump where it had been hacked away only weeks before. The violent act of souvenir hunting had been committed by a *P.I.*-sponsored "Good Will Committee" of "leading Seattle citizens" while on a well-reported excursion of southeast Alaskan ports.

While the committee watched from offshore, third mate R. D. McGillvery took the ship's ax ashore, and later recalled how "The Indians were all away fishing, except for one who stayed in his house and looked scared to death. We picked out the best looking totem pole...I took a couple of sailors ashore

One of Bill Speidel's flock of Seattle Underground tourists poses before the totem.

Right When it was still on Tongass Island, the "Seattle Totem" standing on the far right of this scene, was the most intricately carved column in a crowded beach-front pantheon of totems. Neither was the village "deserted" as Seattle's "goodwill" vandals claimed.

Courtesy of Lawton Gowey

Pioneer Square, circa 1910.

and we chopped it down—just like you'd chop down a tree. It was too big to roll down the beach so we sawed it in two. I got paid $2.50 for the trip which took about two hours." The Tongass Totem was then hoisted aboard the luxury steamer *City of Seattle*, and thereby became the Seattle Totem.

One of those paying McGillvery to chop down the totem and wrestle it aboard was attorney Will H. Thompson. Thompson was the principal speaker at the unveiling, and his rousing oration was a combination of art criticism, amateur anthropology, and heroic denial.

With the latter he met head-on the growing rumor that (to quote him) this "fine heraldic column, born of the romantic Indian thought and fashioned by the cunning of the Indian hand" had been stolen. Thompson countered, "A few fragile folk of over delicate sensibilities have fear that this monument is here as a result of grand larceny. (laughter)...To relieve the oppression upon their minds I will say that the village has long since been deserted...Here the totem will voice the native's deeds with surer speech than if lying prone on moss and fern on the shore of Tongass Island.

Courtesy of Michael Maslan

ONE MORE PUSH—Workers heave to on the totem's base, setting it firmly in the ground. Cement was poured in after | alignment was completed, and guy wires on the tip-top, fifty feet up, will keep the pole from waving in the wind.

NINETY BLAZES BLAMED UPON FIREBUGS HERE

Oct. 22 - 1938

3 More Apartments Added to Criminal Record; Owners Of Homes Told to Be Alert

The mad trail of the arsonists who have menaced Seattle lives and property for the past months is now studded with more than ninety incendiary fires, the fire department disclosed yesterday on the heels of three more fires set in downtown apartment houses.

At the same time Fire Chief William Fitzgerald and Fire Marshal Robert L. Laing disclosed an amazing account of the far-reaching measures taken by the fire department in its unceasing hunt for the mysterious criminal or criminals who have set one blaze after another in Seattle—eighteen in one month.

The three latest fires set by the firebug flared early yesterday in a two-story apartment at 1323 Terry Ave. and at two other apartments, at 1904 Minor Ave. and at 311 E. Pine St. In each instance the fire was discovered before it had spread. Battalion chiefs declared all three blazes were unquestionably the work of firebugs.

MANY QUESTIONED

The investigation in progress for months into the scores of incendiary blazes, as disclosed by the chief and marshal, was all-embracing in its scope.

Salesmen and solicitors, meter readers and deliverymen, and scores of other house-to-house canvassers have been investigated, but none has been found to cover any route on which fires have consistently broken out.

HOME OWNERS WARNED

As many as thirty-five policemen and firemen have been posted at one time in as many different apartment houses to maintain a vigil for the phantom torchmen. Apartment house proprietors have been coached to heed the sound of a fire siren and to immediately investigate their own premises on hearing one, for the reason that the arsonists often set two or three fires in a row, half an hour or less apart.

Firebug Ends Life of Noted Totem Pole

Oct. 23 - 38

Pioneer Square Relic Doomed By Flames

Oct. 23 - 1938

The raven, the frog, the man with the long red nose and other fantastic creatures who compose Seattle's famous totem pole lost a game battle with a firebug in Pioneer Square last night while a thousand spectators looked on.

The firebug struck about 10:15 o'clock. For more than an hour, first smoke, then water poured forth from the eyes of the legendary gods and curled around their feet.

Like that other enemy of the Indian, firewater, the flames gnawed at the pole from inside.

BEAK AMPUTATED

Firemen had difficulty battling the flames which tore at the famous landmark's vitals. They tried to chop a hole at the bottom but failed. Finally, the aerial ladder on truck No. 1 was run up sixty feet and a fireman chopped the beak off the raven to pour water in from the top.

Nobody knows what the firebug had against the historic images, but spectators said they saw a man run up and stuff paper into a hole eaten at the base by dry rot, light it and then flee from sight.

Despite the mutilation, the raven, the frog and the man with the long red nose, who had stood on the same spot since the pole was erected October 18, 1899, maintained traditional Indian stoicism throughout the ordeal. Even their paint appeared unscorched and continued to glisten after the fire was extinguished.

...have to be torn down.

prevention quietly invested in the fire persons the sale of ment.

...ch destroyed 125 1st Ave. ...ed a human ...ess transient building — disclosed the most of the ...ave been in...roy the prop-

we believe ...r three—set in the hall...f apartment ...oms, and in ...ned areas," ...ined.

...re bugs ac...blazing in ...then closed ...to smother

...ng disclosed ...since the in...tarted, they ...g the move-arsonist ...entiaries up ...c Coast, to ...y of them ...the fires. ...trapping the ...he police de...partment is ...ly on the ...tzgerald de...ped, however, ...ut eight fire ...ramped with ...n duties, and ...enty-five fire ...said.

HUNTING!

1938

...lby
...ber down.
...high,
...lanced to see
...he sky.

...ost his back,
...rned pale,
...color black
...ail.

...Chee-cha-co
...and ponder,
...must go
...up yonder.

...Wendell Holmes.

EXPERT ON TOTEM POLES

To The Post-Intelligencer:

From a street car Saturday night I saw flames leaping from the top of our famous sixty-foot Indian-carved totem pole. The firemen had two or three streams drenching the rampant eagle that has perched on the top, holding a three-foot salmon in his talons, for over forty years.

This totem is a historic emblem. If the original cannot be repaired our city should have the Alaska Indians carve a replica to replace it upon the same spot.

The National Furriers Association has adopted the totem as a national emblem. Millions of pictures of Seattle's totem have been sent to all parts of the world.

Another suggestion—if we can get electric light poles put on the handsome concrete balustrades at the foot of each street entering Alaskan Way along our harbor front, each pole to be a facsimile of an Alaska Indian totem pole, say in three or four different designs about six or seven feet above the top railing, this would be the only city in the world with such an attraction. It would put Seattle on the map.

If this could be done early in the ... the poles could be placed ... ghted to be ready for the big ... season that starts here ... It's worth a trial!

...DDY) J. E. STANDLEY, Seattle.

t. 28 - 1938

(applause)" The Seattle-Tongass totem was lowered again 40 years later after a vandal of a less distinguished sort stuffed newspapers into a dryrotting hole near its base, lit them and then ran through a crowd of witnesses who somehow could neither catch the firebug nor dowse the flame. The scarred totem was then shipped north to Alaska where native carvers—some of them related to the Fort Tongass community that years earlier lost their best totem while away fishing—fashioned the replica that now takes the pioneer place of the original.

At the second dedication nothing was officially said of the circumstances surrounding the acquisition of the first totem. But by then it was common knowledge that it had been stolen. Years earlier Thompson and his boys were even fined and paid for what Mrs. Grace Cornish, a passenger on the *City of Seattle*, remembered as an act that "everybody on board treated as a sort of Halloween prank. But I wasn't so sure that it wasn't more serious. I had visited Fort Tongass before that and I found the Indians there proud of their community and its totems."

Courtesy of Don McGaffin

10   Seattle's Sin

In early June, 1986, Bill Speidel's Underground Tours celebrated its 21st anniversary. The first first week of June is also Seattle Fire Week; and the two, the Great Fire of June 6, 1889 and the Seattle underground, are related, as anyone who has either taken Speidel's tour or read his book *Sons of the Profits* will know.

Briefly told, the connection is this. After the fire, the streets in the burned-out Pioneer Square district were raised in some places as much as one story. The old ground level became the new basement, and thus was created the Seattle underground.

Obviously, this interior scene is neither of the city's fire nor its underground, but, rather of its underworld—the higher side of it. And so it is also "about" Bill Speidel who is still the chief chronicler of Seattle's sinful past.

"The Hostess with the Mostest" is the title to the tenth chapter of Speidel's book. Its protagonist, Lou Graham, is

described as "the most important woman in the first fifty years of Seattle's history." That is Madame Graham sitting erect on the left, poised with her employees in the parlor room of "the most glorious and sumptuously furnished palace of sin in the city."

The negative for this rare photograph was uncovered a few years back in a shoe box in a local antique store. The discoverer, Don McGaffin, then still an investigative reporter on King Television's Evening News, borrowed it, printed it, and then called on Speidel. The historian's heart, no doubt, leaped when he first saw this scene plush with its li-bidinous appointments.

Speidel then took McGaffin and the photo to an older expert on the history of local vice, Henry Broderick. The real estate tycoon, then in his nineties, had known Lou Graham (in the course of business) and to Speidel's joy confirmed his hopes and suspicions.

Lou Graham's house (not home) was

at 3rd and Washington. (And it still is, although now filled with lawyers.) She opened in 1888, rebuilt bigger and in brick after the 1889 fire and for another dozen years ran her parlor house in the shadow of City Hall. In fact, Henry Broderick claimed, (borrowing some of Speidel's hyperbolizing over the Madame Graham) that "more city business was transacted at Lou's than at City Hall!"

With the licenses, fees, and payoffs, Graham and her ladies also helped keep the city solvent through the hard times of the mid-1890s. As the rapturous statuary and prints that adorn this parlor reveal, this was a high-class house, and many of the sons of righteous citizens learned something here—as did a few of the righteous themselves.

While for 21 years promoting Seattle's underground, Speidel and his tour leaders have helped preserve its above ground, the historic district around Pioneer Square. Bill Speidel should be thanked and congratulated. Near the ticket window is a blow-up of Madame Graham in her parlor.

Bill Burden

Another scene from the camera of the unidentified photographer seems more familiar than "sinful".

Courtesy of Don McGaffin

"S S Humbolt" Ready to leave for Nome June 2. 1901. Seattle. WA

11 S. S. Humboldt

On June 3, 1901 the *Post-Intelligencer* covered an event that we, through this historical photograph, are witnesses to 85 years later. The newspaper's headline reads, "HUMBOLDT SAILS FOR NOME," and the lead paragraph explains why that disembarking was newsworthy.

"Steamship *Humboldt*, the nineteenth vessel to leave for Nome for the season of 1901 sailed last night at 8 o'clock with 320 passengers and 800 tons of cargo. Not an unoccupied berth or an inch of space for freight remained on the ship, which was first advertised for Nome but a week ago. All of her passenger space was engaged within three days from the date she was announced for the Nome run."

That "Nome run" was the second gold rush north. The first one in 1897, besides the steamship trip north, required an exhausting hike into the inland Yukon. This one, however, was to the beach in front of Nome, and those who stepped aboard the *Humboldt* in Seattle could believe that their next step ashore would be upon the gold-laden ruby sands of Nome. The beaches were open to public digging.

Yet, not everyone on this trip was carrying a shovel. Some on the *Humboldt* were outfitted with back drops and grease paint, for included on the ship's passenger list were 35 members of a theater company booked for Nome's biggest theater, the Standard. "In the crowd," the *P.I.* reported, "are many of the vaudeville stars of the States."

Probably also on board, but hidden, were a few stowaways. The day before, when the steamships *Oregon*, *Centennial* and *Valencia* set out with a total of 1500 passengers bound for Alaska, another *P.I.* story reported that "During the day and on the eve of their departure no less than 100 stowaways were ejected."

The S.S. *Humboldt*'s first Alaskan trip was made for the first rush in 1897 when Seattle's Mayor W. D. Wood resigned his honor and chartered the new wooden steamer for the journey north. For years thereafter, the *Humboldt* was a regular in the Alaska service.

During the 1902 season she returned with three-quarters of a million dollars in gold. However, as Gordon Newell writes

This Seattle goodbye is for the Alaska ferry *Columbia*. Its slip at the foot of Washington St. is but a few blocks south of the *Humboldt's* Arlington Dock departure.

Longtime Ballard resident and sometime deckboy Carl Henry Moen, right, poses with another deckhand aboard the *S.S. Humboldt*. Moen worked aboard the *Humboldt* first in 1911-12 (this trip included) for $25 a month. Later, in 1915-16 his pay was doubled as a quartermaster. (The photo was taken with Moen's camera.)

in his *McCurdy Marine History of the Pacific Northwest*, "There were no bearded miners staggering down the gang plank under the weight of moosehide pokes full of dust and nuggets. Practically all the treasure was from the large gold mining corporations doing business at Dawson and had been produced by machinery rather than by pick, shovel, and pan."

12 The Northern Pacific's New Piers

In their basic shape it's easy to compare this past and present along Alaskan Way. Indeed, the overlapping lines of these three piers are, like fingerprints, patterned so predictably that the two photographers, were they not 85 years apart, might with unamplified voices have discussed—well, the 20th-century fate of Seattle's waterfront.

The historical photographer took his shot about 1902 or shortly after the Northern Pacific Railroad built these three piers between the waterfront feet of Madison and University streets. They were numbered 3 through 5 until the last world war when the military, in the interests of a uniform waterfront, renumbered them 54 through 56.

The railroad's first tenants in Pier 3 were James Galbraith and Cecil Bacon. Their business name appears on the front of Pier 3 below the N.P.'s familiar ying-yang symbol.

Bacon, a chemical engineer with some extra capital, came to Seattle in 1899 and joined Galbraith who had been

selling hay and feed on the waterfront since 1891. Then the Seattle waterfront was still a mess of small pier sheds and shacks supported on timber quays. They were usually set at right angles to the railroad tracks that ran between them and parallel to the waterfront. The gold rush of the late 1890s brought a prosperity to the waterfront that soon rebuilt it.

Here we see the Northern Pacific's part of that new 20th-century waterfront. These sheds conform to the city's new uniform plan for pier alignment. The plan allowed railroads easier access to the sidings and sheds, and it also made it possible to lengthen the wharfs before they reached water too deep to sink timber piles.

When Galbraith and Bacon moved into the new Pier 3, they widened their commercial cast to include building materials. But soon it wasn't hay or lime that called customers to this wharf, but the "Mosquito Fleet." For years this dock was the Elliott Bay home port of the Kitsap Transportation Co. From here

little steamers like the *Hyak*, *Kitsap*, *Reliance*, and *Utopia* steamed away to cross-sound sops like Indianola, Keyport, and Rolling Bay. James Galbraith's son Walter was a director of the Kitsap company.

The ocean steamers that slipped from the sides of Pier 4 (the middle wharf in our scene) were usually steel-hulled and their advertised destinations somewhat more romantic. Signs on the shed's face promoted portage to Antwerp, Havre, London, Cork, Mexico, and San Francisco. Still, in 1902 the gilded romance of Alaska was the larger allure, and from Pier 4 the Alaska Commercial Company's steamers *Portland*, *St. Paul*, and *Bertha* carried the dreamers north to Nome.

Blazoned across the front of the furthest pier (number 5) in this scene is the name Frank Waterhouse. In his day Waterhouse was one of the big names on the waterfront. His steamship line was the first to regularly reach the European Mediterranean from this "Mediterranean of the Pacific," Puget Sound, via Hawaii, the Philippines, Australia, and the Suez Canal. Trade with Russia through Vladivistock was also one of Waterhouse's commercial coups until the 1917 revolution put a stop to that.

Now this old working central waterfront is mostly for playing. And, of course, one of the first players on this strip of import shops and fish bars was Ivar Haglund who in 1938 opened his little aquarium here on Pier 3—now 54. "Hunger" was one of Ivar's stock responses to questions about how he got his start on the waterfront. This commercial appetite was furthered in 1946 when he opened his Acres of Clams restaurant which makes 1986 the 40th anniversary of eating and keeping clam on Pier 54.

Pier 3, now Ivar's Pier 54 since the army renumbered the waterfront during World War 2, was for years the Seattle port for the Kitsap Transportation Co.'s "Mosquito Fleet" steamers like, left to right, the *Magnolia, Florence K* and *Mohawk.*

13   William Hester's Uncommon Vessel

A more typical Hester subject. His customers are in the photo.

In the year of the 1893 financial crash, Ernst and Wilhelm Hester, German immigrant brothers, arrived in Seattle looking for work. They were fortunate and found it as photographers.

The younger brother Wilhelm's specialty was sailing ships. He would read the morning listings of newly-arrived vessels, visit the captains, make arrangements, and return with his bulky 8"x 10" view camera. Technically, his marine photography was excellent, but his subjects were for the most part conventional with shots of the captain, the crew, and the ship. These were the proven sellers, even in depressed times.

This Hester scene, however, is not conventional. And its circumstance is certainly not depressing. The vessel is animated by the two women confidently posing atop its catwalk. And Seattle's turn-of-the-century skyline can be seen through its rigging. The steeple to the left of the mast is Plymouth Congregational Church, then at Third Ave. and University St. The tower to the mast's starboard side sits atop the Arlington Hotel at First and University.

From this setting we can precisely determine in which slip this vessel is harbored. To the right is the old Schwabacker shed at Pier 58. Now its space is part of Waterfront Park. Just out of the picture to the left is the old Pike Street Pier. Today it is part of the Seattle Aquarium. Thus, the two women posing on the ship's catwalk are very near the spot being stepped over by the woman in our "now" view of the park's elevated walkway.

I found this odd Hester in the "Hester-Unidentified" file at the University of Washington's Historical Photography Collection. So did Robert Weinstein, and he included it in *Tall Ships*, his fine book on Hester's work. Although Weinstein was not able to identify this well-kept vessel, he did hazard a picture caption which speculates on the two women before the lens and the man behind it.

He writes, "Wilhelm Hester understood how much newly arrived sailors were starved for female companionship. His shore-side lady friends, ever eager to meet new acquaintances, often accompanied him to the ships even stepping into the picture in coquettish poses on occasion."

Around 1906 Hester stepped out of marine photography and into real estate. He grew moderately wealthy and also a bit eccentric. When he died in 1947, his executor remembered him as a "medium built, thin, clean-shaven man, very stubborn, somewhat parsimonious, and a collector of everything to the point of pathological obsession."

Included in his estate were barrels full of alarm clocks, women's hats, handleless cups, and fortunately, his precious negatives for which he will be forever remembered.

Looking down from the Pike Place Public Market. Hester's subject was docked in the slip between the Schwabacher shed on the left and the Pike St. Wharf.

Courtesy of Harriet Tracy DeLong

14 "Wawona"—The Hoot for Preservation

Pioneer Pacific coast shipbuilder Hans Bendixsen chose the Yosemite Indian word "wawona" to christen the 468-ton schooner of his skilled design that here graces both our "now" and "then." Wawona is the cry an owl makes guarding the forest. That's appropriate, for this schooner was built both of and beside the Pacific forest. It was also first used to haul lumber.

Now decades since its inaugural splash onto California's Humboldt Bay, this softwood schooner holds its three masts high above the southern end of Lake Union. And here another owl-like species of intelligent guardians continue to protect and preserve the *Wawona*—giving a hoot for our maritime heritage.

In 1964 a group of wooden ship enthusiasts decided to save this one and

so formed Save Our Ships. They bought the *Wawona* from a Montana rancher whose plans to fill her holds with Kamchatka-bound cattle fell through.

Between the cattleman and the lumberman, her original owners, the *Wawona* was the property of the Robinson Fisheries Co., which had her working out of Anacortes, then still called by some the "Gloucester of the Pacific." For 30 years, beginning in 1914, the *Wawona* sailed north for codfishing along the Bering Sea slime banks. Fortunately, her inner hull thereby got well pickled and preserved under the weight of the salt-packed codfish.

Another form of preservation for this fortunate ship is Harriet Tracy DeLong's book, *Pacific Schooner, Wawona*. This historical scene is taken

from DeLong's well-constructed history, proceeds from which also go toward preserving the schooner.

This view shows the *Wawona* and the Robinson's tug Challenge tied to the end of the company's codfish-covered Anacortes pier. The now scene reveals the recent and rare reunion of the old schooner and her even older tug. They lie alongside one another at the Wawona's Lake Union slip beside the Center for Wooden Boats.

Built in 1890 the Tug *Challenge* was sometimes used to tow the Wawona out the straits to the Pacific breezes or into Ballard for winter moorage. Ken De Nike, the *Challenge*'s present owner, has

Harriet Tracy DeLong poses with her book at the entrance to the *Wawona's* galley.

beautifully restored her.

In 1970 the *Wawona* was declared a national historic site, the first vessel so distinguished. For the more than 20 years since they first purchased the *Wawona*, Northwest Seaport has continued to save our ship with volunteer labor. This difficult and actually endless labor of preserving the schooner's historical wooden soul is really a spiritual service for all who wish to step aboard more than the merely sterile and inert convenience of fiberglass.

The Pacific schooner *Wawona* is open for public pleasure on weekends, and the book *Wawona* is available on board.

Heading out from Ballard.

Courtesy of Washington State Historical Society

15 Fly on the *Flyer*

Colman Dock has been built and rebuilt six times: twice before the Great Fire of 1889 and four times after. This, its fourth incarnation, was constructed in 1908—but not all of it. This tower, its second, came later.

The original belfry (pictured in the next story) was a participant in the most dramatic docking collision in the history of Elliott Bay when on the night of April 25, 1912 the ocean liner, *Alameda* sliced clean through Colman dock and dropped its original tower into the bay. The steel-hulled *Alameda* was barely scratched.

In this photograph the dock's replacement tower is almost brand new. The evidence for that comes from the second pile behind it. In 1913 the Smith Tower's terra-cotta skin was completed to its pyramidal top. Here, on the right, it's almost there. For nearly a quarter-century these were twin-towers to the millions of

Top The second Colman tower under construction and *bottom* in a temporary condition of deconstruction while the threatening flames from the Grand Trunk Fire lick across the slip.

"Mosquito Fleet" passengers that plied the waters of Elliott Bay enroute to the many docking stations along the 705-ft. sides of Colman Dock. But long before this ornate skyline signaled to commuters and tourists on Puget Sound, a greater symbol of the Sound had been "flying" over it for more than 20 years.

The stern of the sleek steamer *Flyer* is the foremost subject in this scene. Beginning regularly in 1892, "Fly on the Flyer" was the celebrated prescription for a speedy steam between Seattle and Tacoma. It was Puget Sound's busiest run, and the *Flyer* dominated it with her speed. By 1908, the year this Colman Dock was built, she had already carried over 3 million passengers on what some wit calculated amounted to 53 circum-navigations of the globe or five trips to the moon, burning 24 cords of wood a day.

The ferry *Walla Walla*, easing into the latest—sixth—Colman Dock in the contemporary photograph, and the little *Flyer* might be compared. When completed in 1972, the *Walla Walla* and her sister ship the *Spokane* were the biggest double-ended ferries in the world. For most of her years she's been running loops between Seattle and Winslow at a fast clip approaching 18 knots. Of course, she has no competitors, while the Flyer was constantly having to prove her primacy by leaving challengers in her wake. Now if the *Flyer* were to race the *Walla Walla* from Colman Dock to Eagle Harbor, she could run at least one circle around her and still win the race to Winslow.

And the *Flyer* was famous not only for her dependable speed but also for her smooth vibrationless ride. She barely kicked up a wake. The *Walla Walla* was first designed to pack tourists about the San Juan Islands. After four months she was kicked off the islands, in part, because of the "tidal waves" she ploughed out of the Sound crashed with such energy against the island's shores that the flimsier cottages there were endangered at high tide.

The *Flyer* was the second most famous ship to regularly course these waters. The first, of course, was the *Kalakala*. When "The World's First Streamlined Ferry" was introduced in 1935, her modern sides were a perfect compliment to the new art deco Colman Dock (number five) then being designed and completed, sans tower, in 1937.

But of all the historic steamers shown here the one to serve the longest on these waters was the *City of Everett*. Her stern's showing on the left. Built in 1900 for the Seattle-Everett run she concluded her service as the Four Winds Restaurant on Lake Union, only going down when her pumps failed after City Light turned off the power for failure to pay on a delinquent bill.

For many early-century years Ye Olde Curiosity Shop was in the Colman Dock.

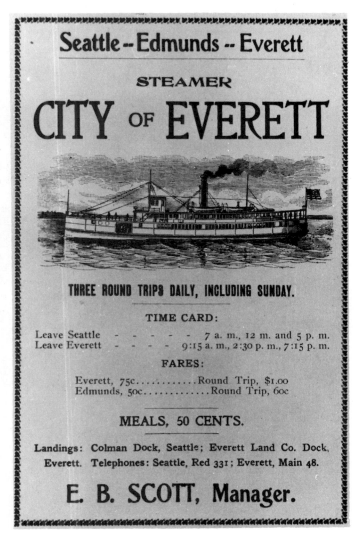

Seattle -- Edmunds -- Everett

STEAMER
CITY OF EVERETT

THREE ROUND TRIPS DAILY, INCLUDING SUNDAY.

TIME CARD:

Leave Seattle - - - - - - 7 a. m., 12 m. and 5 p. m.
Leave Everett - - - - - 9:15 a. m., 2:30 p. m., 7:15 p. m.

FARES:

Everett, 75c.............Round Trip, $1.00
Edmunds, 50c.............Round Trip, 60c

MEALS, 50 CENTS.

Landings: Colman Dock, Seattle; Everett Land Co. Dock, Everett. Telephones: Seattle, Red 331; Everett, Main 48.

E. B. SCOTT, Manager.

TRANSPORTATION DEPARTMENT
POLK'S SEATTLE CITY DIRECTORY—1909. 1807

L. B. SEELEY, President and General Manager, Portland, Ore.
S. H. BROWN, Jr., Vice-President, Boston, Mass.
E. W. CRICHTON, Secretary and Treasurer, Portland, Ore.
URI SEELEY, Agent, Seattle, Wash.

Columbia River and Puget Sound Navigation Company

FAST STEAMER
FLYER
BETWEEN SEATTLE AND TACOMA

FLY ON THE FLYER
SEATTLE TO TACOMA. ONE HOUR AND TWENTY-FIVE MINUTES

LANDINGS:
N. P. Wharf, Tacoma; Flyer Dock, Seattle

Courtesy of University of Washington Historical Photography Collection

16   At the Foot of Madison

Besides being pictorially pleasing, this waterfront scene is crowded with history, and all of it is either afloat or on timber pilings. At the foot of Madison St., it is the site of Fire Station #5; the far left of the historical photo reveals some of the station.

The fireboat *Duwamish* is warming up at the end of the station's short pier. Built in 1909 at Richmond Beach for the Seattle Fire Dept., the 113-ft-long *Duwamish* weighed a relatively heavy 309 tons. (In 1984 it was replaced by the new fireboat, *Chief Seattle*, and so just missed making it into both our photos.) The smoke that escapes from its twin stacks partially obscures the tower of the Grand Trunk Pacific Dock.

The Grand Trunk Pacific was Canada's second transcontinental railroad. After reaching its terminus, Prince Rupert, in 1910, it took up the steamship business as well running a coastal feeder service from Seattle, Victoria and Vancouver to Prince Rupert.

In its time, the Grand Trunk pier was the largest wood structure of its kind on the West Coast, but its time was brief. On July 29, 1914, it was gutted by the second most dramatic fire in the city's

history. (The first, of course, was the Great Fire of 1889.) Sitting next door to Station #5 did not save it, although their fireboats *Duwamish* and *Snoqualmie* did

help keep the Grand Trunk fire to itself.

The probable year for this photograph is 1910. Then the *Duwamish* was only one year old and the Puget Sound steamer *Inland Flyer* (on the right), after 11 years of running on what was called the "Navy Yard Route" to Port Orchard, was sold to a Captain R. G. Reeve who changed its name to *Mohawk*. Here, *Inland Flyer* is still inscribed on the bow.

This little 106-ft-long wooden steamer was only 7 ft. shorter than the fireboat, but at 151 tons was less than half as heavy. In 1916 Captain Reeves ignobly stripped it of its engine and converted it into a fish barge at Neah Bay. But here moored at the Galbraith Dock, Pier 3, it is still a working member of the "Mosquito Fleet" of small steamers plying Puget Sound.

Pier 3—long since renumbered Pier 54—is the only survivor from the "then" into the "now" (except, of course, the fireboat which moved on but may return as a waterfront museum.) For nearly 50 years, first as an aquarium and then as a fish bar, it has been the platform for Ivar Haglund's prescriptions to "keep clam!" And, although the late Ivar Haglund just missed seeing his remodeled Acres of Clams reopened, he did help choose the scores of historical waterfront photographs that now cover the Acres' walls.

One of his favorites was a blow-up of this historical photo. It is actually one of many Seattle images recently uncovered in northern Idaho—far from clams—and now hanging in the Acres. One of Ivar's last philanthropic acts was to help purchase this collection for the University of Washington's Historical Photography Collection.

Fireboats *Duwamish*, left and *Snoqualmie*, right, rest in their slips before the old clapboard Station #5, ca 1911. *Below* the view up Madison from the second floor of the fire station.

Courtesy of Lawton Gowey

The old red brick Station #5 was unfortunately sacrificed to the modern prefabricated look of the contemporary station at the foot of Madison St.

Courtesy of University of Washington Historical Photography Collection

Courtesy of Old Seattle Paperworks, Pike Place Market

17   The *Iroquois* and its Chief Steward

This "now" image was NOT taken from the same place as the "then" but from as near to it as one might safely and comfortably reach on a rainy day without a row boat.

The historical image is part of a recently uncovered collection of negatives most of which date from 1910. That is also the year of Jack Dillon's birth, and here—in our contemporary photograph—he stands at the south end of Pier 54 and points towards the site from which the photographer, unknown to us now, "captured" the steamer *Iroquois* tied up along the north side of Colman Dock and taking on passengers.

Just north of the Colman Dock was the Grand Trunk Pacific Pier. It also had its tower and was another terminal for the busy "Mosquito Fleet" of small steamers then swarming the sound. Very near where the *Yakima* is seen disembarking from the northern slip of the present-day ferry terminal is the spot where the Grand Trunk pier extended its farthest into the bay. It is there that the photographer set his camera and aimed it directly south at the Colman tower. In 1964 when both piers were razed for the wider but stubbier Washington State Ferries Terminal the towers were already long gone, but their imposing presentation to the bay is preserved for us still in photographs like these.

Jack Dillon's ties to the *Iroquois* are

far more close-knit than the coincidence of his and the photograph's birth. In 1910 his father, Jack Sr., was working on the *Iroquois* as chief steward. It is an engaging possibility that his father was on board ship attending to the care and comfort of its passengers as it was being photographed here. In that era of labor relations there were no days off. If Mrs. Dillar and the baby wished to spend some time with Dad, they did it on board.

Jack Jr. took his first ride on the *Iroquois* round trip to Vancouver at the age of two weeks. His last trip aboard ship was in 1936, and like his father before him, he served it as chief steward. But the ship had changed. In 1927 the *Iroquois* had been radically redesigned for passengers who were in the habit of taking their automobiles with them. Large barn-like doors were cut into its bow and a center corridor was cleared for cars. The age of elegant steaming was giving way to that of bridges, paved roads, and the dangerous convenience of automobiles.

In 1907 when the *Iroquois* first "came around" from the Great Lakes for its Puget Sound service, water transportation was still an exhilarating opportunity to have someone else do the driving while you enjoyed the scenery or rested in your stateroom. The *Iroquois* could carry about 800 passengers and a crew of about 30. A one-way trip to Vancouver cost three dollars. A year later, in 1908, the price for the similar trip to Victoria crashed to 25 cents. The Black Ball Line fell into a price war with the Canadian Pacific's competing steamer service. Luckily for profits they managed to again fix prices in time for the 1909 Alaska Yukon and Pacific Exposition.

In 1910 the departure time for the normal run to Vancouver was 8:15. In our photograph the tower clock reads almost nine, the passengers are lounging on deck and the flags are out. All this suggests to Jack Dillon that the *Iroquois* might very well here be readying for a Sunday excursion to the ocean and back.

The Colman clock reached its last hour on the night of April 25, 1912 when Capt. "Dynamite" John O'Brien, while preparing to dock his huge ocean-going *Alameda*, commanded the ship engineer to give a routine "full-speed astern" and was answered with a "full-speed ahead" instead. The ship crashed through the tower. The sternwheeler *Telegram* which was lying along the north side of the dock was rammed and pushed into the adjacent Grand Trunk pier. The *Telegram* sank; the tower stayed afloat in the bay and the *Alameda* backed out with hardly a scratch.

Two years later on July 3O, 1914 the Grand Trunk tower met a similar fate but by more common means. Our third photograph shows three Seattle landmarks in a line. The just-completed Smith Tower on the left and the second Colman tower on the right frame the sensational demise of the Grand Trunk Pier. It was rebuilt, but this time without the tower.

The last time Jack Dillon saw the *Iroquois*, in 1972, it was laid up in Lake Union. "Little Jack," the son of "Big Jack," had grown up to become a vice president for Alaska Steamship Co. and then regional manager of Alaska for the Port of Seattle. When he retired in 1976, the *Iroquois* had already been out three

"Telegraph" at Colman Dock Seattle.

The *Telegraph* nestles along the north side of Colman Dock where she was later sunk when the steel-hulled *Alameda* crashed through the wharf.

Courtesy of Museum of History and Industry

years in Alaskan waters processing king crab.

Many groups are active in preserving access to our region's maritime history and the living memories that freely circulate about the waterfront. These include Puget Sound Maritime

Historical Society, Northwest SeaPort, and Waterfront Awareness whose book, *Seattle's Waterfront*, deserves a good reading. Jack Dillon and many others are active in this work of nurturing our community's vital connections between "now" and "then."

18   The Sidewheeler *George E. Starr*

The first time the *George E. Starr*, a locally build sidewheeler, backed out into Elliott Bay on August 12, 1879, the entire city was either on board or at shore. The occasion was no ordinary ship launching; the *Starr* with its 154-ft. length and 28-ft. beam, was then the largest vessel built on Puget Sound.

The historic launching site was at the foot of Cherry St. A band played and the crowd cheered as the *Starr* was knocked loose, but the din suddenly dropped dead when the sidewheeler got stuck in her skids. She was comically rocked free when those on board ran back and forth, in unison, from one side of the ship to the other. It was reported that in this rocking release several passengers got seasick and one man fell overboard.

Except for a brief stint on the Columbia River (running between Astoria and Ilwaco) and hauling men and horses to Skagway (in 1897 for the Klondike gold rush), the *Starr* spent its remaining

The steamer *Dode.* *Courtesy of University of Washington Historical Photography Collection*

years competing on Puget Sound for freight and passengers. She is pictured here around the turn of the century backing out of her slip near the foot of Main St. Twenty-five years old, the ship was slow for the times. Much of her business was lost to sternwheelers, ships with steel hulls and screw propellers, and, of course, to trains.

When the *Starr* was retired in 1911, she was the last sidewheeler on Puget Sound (aside from the ferries to West Seattle.) Her last months were spent tied to a buoy in the harbor where she was used as a temporary storehouse for powder and explosives which could not be brought onto the waterfront after dark.

The Starr's *most* volatile mission, however, was the three-mile race she ran against another steamship, the *Dode,* in 1902. Both ships left the Whatcom dock in the evening headed for Fairhaven. The race soon developed into a pounding as the bigger *Starr* attempted to push the *Dode* ashore. While the *Starr*'s officers yelled assurances at the paying customers, the passengers were not comforted. Many yelled protests at Capt. Gunder Hansen for "willfully jeopardizing our lives."

One passenger, Dan Mulligan, announced he was getting off the boat because of the election in Seattle and, being a Democrat, he felt the party needed him. Several others disembarked with him at Fairhaven and completed the trip to Seattle by rail.

Building the *G.E.Starr's* hull at the foot of Cherry Street., 1879. *Courtesy of Seattle Public Library*

The *G.E.Starr* at another Seattle pier.

Courtesy of University of Washington Historical Photography Collection

19 Seattle's *Nebraska*

In the fall of 1904 while Teddy Roosevelt was campaigning for re-election on his record of big stick diplomacy with gunboats, Seattle was building its own gunboat, the battleship *Nebraska*.

At precisely ten minutes after two on the afternoon of October 8, Miss Mary Mickey, the daughter of Nebraska Governor John Mickey, broke a bottle of wine against the dreadnought's red steel bow. The front page lead story of the next day's *Seattle Times* described what followed.

"Majestically and with the power of newly-created life, the battleship *Nebraska* was launched from the ways of the Moran Bros. shipyards...amidst hurrahs from 60,000 throats, the blowing of sirens and whistles, the reverberating of booms...and the inspiring strains of the national anthem from a half dozen bands. The newest of Uncle

Sams' fighting machines was consigned to the bosom of the mighty deep...the bubbling wine christening it to a career of usefulness in preserving the peace of the world and the integrity of the nation."

The *Times* described it as a "red-letter day in Seattle's history," and Asahel Curtis captured it photographically at its most exhilarating moment. In this picture one can still hear the roar of the crowds that cram the docks to either side of the "monster fighting craft... Moran's masterpiece." A day earlier, the city's newspapers published a "Warning to People." Included was the notice, "it is declared to be dangerous to go out on the wharves...no vessels are allowed on the bay at a distance 1000 ft. from where the battleship rests." The warning predicted that "The plunge of the *Nebraska* will raise a tidal wave."

At the moment of the launch both the piers and the bay were crammed with enthusiasts willing to live dangerously. The *Times* reported, "So great a number of water craft was never seen before in the harbor." Since no accidents were reported, we may conclude that the row boat in the right foreground of Curtis' scene survived the wake. Rather, everyone was "surprised by the smoothness of the launching" as this "heretofore inanimate centaur of the sea swept away from

LAUNCHING OF THE

BATTLESHIP NEBRASKA

THE launching of the Battleship Nebraska from Moran Brothers shipyard next Friday marks the culmination of an epoch in Seattle's manufacturing interests. It is a time of triumph not alone for the shipbuilding firm but as well for the city at large which has contributed so liberally through its leading business men to the successful initiation and completion of the work. On the day

MR. ROBERT MORAN
President of Moran Bros. Company

of launching a check for $100,000, representing the total amount pledged by public spirited citizens of Seattle to secure the award of the Nebraska contract to a local firm, will be presented to Mr. Robert Moran as part of the ceremonies. Viewed from every standpoint the launching is one of the most significant events in the history of this city and will attract the attention of the country to the queen city of Puget Sound.

The Moran Bros. Company
requests the pleasure of your company at the Launching of the
United States Battleship "Nebraska"
Friday, the seventh of October, nineteen hundred and four
at two thirteen o'clock, p. m.
Christened by Miss Mary Rain Mickey

the speaker's stand, and, in the ecstasy of a glorious freedom, settled down into the waves with hardly a quiver."

The economic wave was felt for years as Seattle, during the course of the First World War developed into one of the country's largest launchers of gunboats.

Courtesy of Michael Maslan

During and just after the parade, as seen from the Second Ave. side of the Seattle Hotel. (see story #8)

20 The Visit of T.R.'s Fleet

The old Haller building at Second Ave. and Columbia St. was photographed here in the afternoon of May 26, 1908. That was time enough for the day's "mighty throng" to have dispersed after "the biggest pageant ever seen in Seattle had passed before it."

That morning's three-mile-long military parade was the last big hurrah of a four-day event which started on Saturday with the arrival all-in-a-row into Elliott Bay of 13 battleships from Theodore Roosevelt's Great White Fleet.

For this, the *Post-Intelligencer* reported, "Seattle never before in its history appeared in such gay attire." The Haller Building was reviewed as "decorated in a tasteful and artistic manner." But it was a modest adornment compared to some of the garnishing done by businesses along the parade route. The *P.I.* story continued, "Vying with one another the mercantile firms have created a veritable spasm of color on First, Second and Third avenues...the eye almost wearies of the view."

The Alaska Building at 14 stories, the city's first skyscraper, was adorned with more than 500 flags. A block south of the Haller at Cherry St., became at night a target for a barrage of spotlights shot from the "thirteen great fighting machines" in Elliott Bay.

Throughout these four days, Seattle was in the center of two tides. From the

west came the dreadnoughts and from all other directions came an estimated 200 thousand visitors who, the *P.I.* reported, took the city "by storm. Night and day the streets are full, alive with a rushing tide of humanity restless as the sea."

And the next day, Wednesday, May 27, Teddy Roosevelt's big show moved on to Tacoma for four more days of boat races, parades, barbecues, dress balls, and buildings dressed in the "color emblems which a patriotic people revere."

Courtesy of Bill Greer

21 Central School

Throughout the 1860s and 70s, the Territorial University on Denny's Knoll, the present site of the Olympic Hotel, was the crowning landmark on the city's horizon.

During the winter of 1882-83, the focus shifted two blocks east and two blocks south, as the great white wooden hulk of the new Central School was raised in the block bordered by 6th and 7th avenues, and Madison and Marion streets.

With six rooms on each of its two floors and another two stories of tower above, it was the largest school in Washington Territory. It could seat 800 students. Yet, this crowning glory was shortlived. In the spring of 1888 the Central School burned to the ground.

The five years the school was around covered a time of radical change for Seattle. The new Central School was opened in a small town where the familiarity of everything and everyone was fast fading. On January 14, 1882 citizens gathered in Yesler Hall to vote for the speedy construction of the new schoolhouse. Three days later many of the same grassroots, civic-minded agitators pulled from the city jail two prisoners accused

of murdering a local businessman named Reynolds. After encouraging a confession, the crowd lynched them on two maples along Yesler Way.

During the next few years familiar faces were crowded by strangers. By 1889 outsiders were coming in on the

transcontinental Northern Pacific at a rate of 1,000 a month. From 1880 to 1890 a city anxious to attract immigrants, yet fearful of strangers, had grown from 4,000 to 40,000.

For Seattle, the 1880s was a decade of growing pains. It faced racial resentment like the anti-Chinese riots of 1886, technological innovations like the telephone, public transportation and a general electric lighting system, and

physical devastation like the Great Fire of 1889.

So the April 1888 burning of the wood-frame Central School was a temporary sensation upon the scene of a community busy at becoming a big city. Within a year a new brick Central School was built on the same site. For a time it also dominated the city's skyline.

The historical scene was photographed from near the southern side of James St.'s intersection with Seventh Ave. Thus, in the contemporary view from the Yesler Way Interstate-5 overpass, we are looking over the historical photographer's shoulder. If it were still around, Central School would sit in the center of the southbound lanes of the freeway, from this point of view partially hidden by the Madison St. exit sign.

Although dominated by Central School, this old cityscape reveals many other features of 1888. To the immediate left of the schoolhouse, at the southeast corner of Sixth Ave. and Marion St. is the Joseph McNaught mansion. On the right, Seventh Ave. is interrupted at Columbia St. which makes a smooth transection of the entire scene because it was recently regraded.

On the lower left is a topographical oddity which has since been regraded.

Courtesy of Seattle Public Library

There, Cherry St. actually descends to the east from Sixth Ave. before rising again at the alley for its final ascent of First Hill. An elevated boardwalk allows pedestrians to pass over the depression.

Further to the west, at the present site of the Federal Courthouse, the center tower of Providence Hospital punctures the horizon. To its left is the Territorial University with its roof balustrade and simple cupola. Behind these landmarks are the lightly populated and as yet unleveled Denny Hill, and beyond that the hazy horizon of Magnolia. The timber stand on the far right of the photo is Queen Anne Hill.

Courtesy of University of Washington Historical Photography Collection

Comparing this view of Central School with that on the facing page will allow the curious among you to figure approximately from where the other shot was taken.

22 David Judkin's "Outside Work"

David Roby Judkins, pioneer photographer of this historical scene, ran a short advertisement in the August 26, 1886 *Post-Intelligencer* "offering his patrons first-class cabinets at $2.50 a dozen." These cabinets were not pieces of furniture, but the then-popular photographic print size that measured 4½-by-6½ inches. Judkins' offer was a good one; in fact, it was too good.

One week later, on September 3, Judkins and his three principal Seattle competitors, George Moore, Theodore E. Peiser and M. S. McClaire met for a little price fixing. Together they ran a *P.I.* ad under the resolute headline, NOTICE. They announced, "We, the UNDER-SIGNED PHOTOGRAPHERS, have decided that the present prices for photographs are below those of other reputable galleries in other cities, and have concluded to act in concert and harmony, and ask a more reasonable recompense for our skill and labor."

From then on the quartet would charge five dollars a dozen for cabinet prints. And in this agreement they assured Seattle "we pledge our honor to sustain, and politely request the public not to ask us to deviate from the same as our determination is unalterable and just."

After years of successful photography in Kansas City, D. R. Judkins arrived in Seattle in 1883. He settled into a studio at Second Ave. and Columbia St. and from there sold more than cabinet cards. A typical Judkins advertisement offered to "mount your portrait in a pin, ring or locket" or on the popular and cheaper carte-de-visite wallet-sized prints.

Although his bread-and-butter was probably portraits, Judkins "paid particular attention to outside work" offering "views of Seattle and surrounding country." This historical photograph is one of these outside views of Seattle.

Although probably not among his best sellers, it is still very revealing of a part of the city rarely photographed in the 1880s.

Judkins shot this scene from the roof of Central School at Sixth Ave. and Madison St. (A little of the top trim of that landmark's north gable rises into the photo's lower left-hand corner.) With this scene Judkins looked away from the city's center, and north towards the still forested Queen Anne Hill on the left and the rough shores of Lake Union on the right. The intersection of 7th Ave. and Spring is in the right foreground.

Central School opened May 7, 1883. Then the largest school in Washington Territory, for five years it dominated the Seattle horizon. Seattle was growing so explosively through the 1880s that the school was soon crowded and, as this photo begins to reveal, so was the neighborhood north of it.

Above The new Central School from the corner of Seventh Ave. and Madison Street.

Looking down on the old Central School from near the corner of Ninth Ave. and Columbia Street. Compare this photo to those on the preceeding pages.

Courtesy of Lawton Gowey

23 James McNaught and the Collected Poems of Percy Bysshe Shelley

When local book lovers met at Yesler's Hall in August 1868 to organize Seattle's first library association, they appointed Sara Yesler librarian. On the executive board's list of classic titles for acquisition were Ralph Waldo Emerson's *Essays*, William Cullen Bryant's *Thanatopsis*, and Percy Shelley's *Collected Poems*. But one board member objected to the latter selection, calling the poet a "freethinker." Fortunately for freethinking, this objection was overruled. (Living today, that board member would probably call Shelley a "secular humanist.")

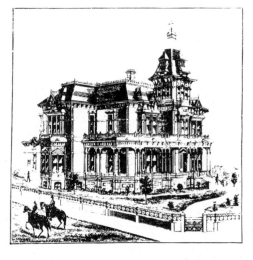

One board member who was probably an advocate of Shelly was the association's first president, James McNaught, an erudite young lawyer with bad eyes and thick lenses. Whatever McNaught read, including romantic poets, he held it four inches from his face.

When McNaught had arrived in town only one year earlier, he created quite a sensation with his exceedingly high silk hat and long frock coat. McNaught's cosmopolitan costume fit neither his new hometown of rough-palmed stump pullers nor his own financial condition. The dapper young McNaught had only enough cash to pay for one week's board, and no prospects. However, he kept wearing that hat and coat, and 22 years later McNaught was working in New York City as Northern Pacific Railroad's chief solicitor and commuting to his high-fashion home on the Hudson River near West Point. When he left his Seattle home on Fourth Ave., he held a high place among the legal fraternity of Washington Territory.

Courtesy of Seattle Engineering Dept.

Here we see the effects of a nitrate negative going bad. But this contact print from the Seattle Engineering Department's priceless photographic collection is still such a dignified setting of the old Carnegie Library's steps and the McNaught mansion's tower beyond them, that it deserves a showing—splotches and streaks or no.

The home James and Agnes McNaught and their two children left behind in Seattle is the mansion prominent in the primary historical photograph. Built at the southeast corner of Fourth Ave. and Spring St. in 1883 for $50,000, it was a monument to the entrepreneur who built it and designed to be conspicuously included in all the local tour books. A home like this one required servants, and there were three or four rooms for everyone. The sumptuous display of furnishings cost nearly as much as the many wings, gables, and towers that sheltered them.

At about the same time McNaught left town, his old friends and associates started a new social organization they called the Rainier Club. Their purpose was to further nurture the success of their "Seattle Spirit" by promoting their social and business connections. The club's first home was the McNaught mansion where it stayed until 1893 when it was converted into a boarding house.

By 1904 the city had bought the entire block of the mansion site to put up the local library's first permanent home. The photograph looking across Fourth Ave. from the present location of the Seafirst Building was most likely taken some time shortly before the big

Top Two scenes of the McNaught Mansion at its new location across Spring St. *Below that* the ruins of the Seattle Public Libary, and the McNaught's Mansion at its original and future SPL site.

house was moved across Spring St. to the northeast corner of its intersection with Fourth Ave. A small portion of the mansion's southern side is revealed at the far left of the second historical photograph. It focuses on the new Carnegie Library, taken soon after it was completed in 1907.

The Carnegie Library was built with a $220,000 donation from Andrew Carnegie, steel magnate and philanthropist. Considered the most distinguished structure in town, 50 years later it was described by Kenneth Colman, chairman of the citizens for the library bond issue, as "a community eyesore, not fit for a progressive and forward looking city like Seattle." The bond issue passed, and by 1957 the same forces of local modernism that gave us a municipal building and Public Safety Building that look like airport hotels, were at work on the new library, the one seen over the Moore sculpture in the contemporary photograph. Fortunately the quality of modernism involved in the new library is from some perspectives pleasing enough, whereas those other municipal piles left us by the 50s are depressing from any prospect. Henry Moore's "Vertebrae" (seen in the "now" photo) was an expression of a different sort of organic modern, for which the city, if it lets it slip away, will show the lack of another kind of vertebrae.

In the oldest image, behind the McNaught mansion we can see the center tower and southern half of Providence Hospital at the present location of the Federal Courthouse at Fifth Ave. and Madison St. To the right of the hospital and one block east at Sixth Ave. rise the brick towers of Central School that was completed in 1889.

The buildings in these historical scenes are long gone. Providence Hospital moved to its present location at 17th Ave. and East Jefferson St. in 1911. Central School was leveled in August 1953. The McNaught residence was replaced by the Hotel Hungerford, and the distinguished but inadequate and unsafe Carnegie Library was leveled in 1956. However, there's still some continuity with those first library association meetings where McNaught presided in 1868. Shelley's poetry has neither been expunged nor outmoded.

Courtesy of Seattle Public Library

Top In the late 1940s, Seattle's first Modern government building, the Federal Court House took the site of the old Providence Hospital which had long since move to its present location.

Courtesy of Mrs Herbert Coe

24 First Hill Home

Although it is not an historical event, here is a candid canine moment on Seattle's First Hill, circa 1895. The leaping dog in the historical photo's foreground upsets the two girls, center and right. They are recoiling, but the girl on the left seems lost in a contemplation of her opened hands. Has the dog just jumped from her caress? Or has he just bitten or scratched her?

Behind this quartet is the home of the James Campbell family at 1119 James St., on the southwest corner of James and Minor. The Campbells' two daughters, Jessie and Lucy, (center and right, respectively) were born and grew up here.

The family's huge front lawn was one of the neighborhood's most popular playgrounds—not for the polite adult recreations like tennis and crochet (for those there were courts nearby)—but for

the creative play of First Hill's children and dogs. This grassy expanse filled the block west to Boren Ave., and so was long enough for football. Lucy Campbell, for nearly 70 years now Mrs. Herbert Coe, recalls that "The boys were always kicking that ball around," and every autumn muddying up the lawn.

In this scene Lucy, her sister Jessie, and, examining her hands, the daughter of a family friend from California sit on the dry grass near the center of the lawn. Today they would be sitting to the right of where in the "now" photo the car sits in the parking lot behind the Minor and James Medical Center.

James Campbell was a pioneer Seattle hardwareman who, at the age of seven, migrated with his family from the Scottish Island of Isley first to Canada, and then, as a young man on his own, to Seattle. By the mid-1870s he was selling miners outfits and anvils from his Union Hardware at First and Marion. His business prospered, and the Campbells were soon ready to build their home on the hill and raise a family. They moved in shortly after their first-born, Dudley arrived in 1883. Theirs was an early residence in a neighborhood that during the 1890s would fill up with fashionable mansions.

Jessie Campbell followed in 1885. Lucy, the youngest Campbell was born here in 1887 and lived at 1119 James St. until she married the late Dr. Herbert Coe, former chief of staff at Children's Orthopedic Hospital. For nearly 70 years, she has lived in their Washington Park home, and is now surrounded by flowers, family, and the appointments of nearly 98 years.

Although Lucy Campbell Coe cannot recall who took this candid shot of her first home, she does remember the name of the family dog, but cannot now imagine why he was called Lee Hung Chang.

Top Lucy Campbell plays with the cat beside the family home. The Phinney house (of the ridge and Woodland Park) is behind her. *Center* The Campbell front lawn and home shows to the left of the grander Lippy residence at James and Boren. The smokestack of the James St. powerhouse is also evi-dent on the left. *Bottom* The author visits with Lucy Coe over tea and family photos in her front room.

25 Castlemount

In 1883 the old Indian fighter Colonel Granville O. Haller retired from the service and built himself a mansion. It was the first on Seattle's First Hill—a neighborhood that would soon become the city's first high-class community. The Hallers called their home "Castlemount," and its towering bulk did not so much grace the ridge behind Seattle as dominate it.

Pioneer Seattle historian Clarence Bagley's description of the colonel's physiognomy suits the facade of his home as well. "His broad brow indicated a strong intellect, his eye shone clear and bright and he was never afraid to look any man in the face." We can imagine the wide-eyed military man alert in his tower atop the "broad brow" of his castle and looking most of Seattle in the face.

After fighting the Seminoles in Florida and the Mexicans in Mexico City, the heroic Haller first came to the Northwest in 1853 to hunt down and sometimes hang insurrecting Indians.

Ten years later, in 1863, while fighting in the Civil War on the Union side, Haller at a wine-tasting party with a few light-headed officers, made an impru -

dent but ambiguous remark that might have included Lincoln's name. A navy man absurdly twisted the incident and had Haller dismissed without a hearing for the "uttering of disloyal sentiments."

Haller fled his "unjust disgrace," came west again and settled first on

Whidbey Island to raise a family. It took him 16 years to gain by joint resolution of Congress "complete exoneration," and reinstatement with the rank of colonel, but in those years he managed to also raise a sizable fortune on Puget Sound. A model of pioneer enterprise, he worked it all—real estate, lumbering, farming, and general merchandising—out of a Coupeville store front.

Very well off, Granville Haller and his wife Henrietta lived together in their Castlemount for 14 years, until the colonel's death in 1897. By then they were surrounded by mansions but none of them reached the almost monolithic height of Castlemount.

Henrietta died in 1910, and the Haller's son Theodore was left to watch over (and down from) what in his tenure became known as the "Ghost House." It seemed particularly haunted to Theodore's wife Constance.

When they were married in 1917, Theodore was an 53-year-old career businessman, obsessed with frugally managing his sizable inheritance. Constance was 30 years his junior, and after 11 years in the mansion, wife had husband in the divorce court complaining that she had to wear clothes inferior to her station, drive a second-hand automobile, and live in that great ghost house.

And Judge Ronald agreed. Granting the divorce he sympathetically concluded that "It was not pleasant for a young

Above This copy of a torn print shows the Haller mansion to the left of a James St. Cable Car and the cable line's powerhouse at Broadway. *Below* This panoramic view from the Coppin's watertower at 9th and Columbia shows the first rather treeless bloom of the First Hill neighborhood. The dominant Castlemount is on the left, and to its right (and marked by the arrow) is the Campbell residence featured in the preceeding story.

woman to be alone in that house day after day with nothing to look forward to but a game of dominoes in the evening. The mansion was once the finest in Seattle, its gingerbread scroll work highly regarded, and its furnishings considered the last work in luxury. But its windows did rattle, its floors were warped and cold. Naturally, Haller didn't notice it—he was used to the house. Mrs.

Haller was not."

The inconstant Constance was awarded a $30,000 settlement and within two years Theodore was dead. The mansion was eventually razed, the property leveled, and during World War II the government leased the grounds and put up a temporary and decidedly unluxurious housing project of five buildings with eight apartments each—for 40 families.

Courtesy of University of Washington Historical Photography Collection

Courtesy of Michael Maslan

26 Society Tennis

Under the headline "FIRST DAY OF TENNIS," the Post-Intelligencer for July 25, 1895 predicted, "What is likely to prove the most successful as it certainly is the largest tennis tournament ever held in the Northwest began yesterday noon on the grounds of the Olympic Tennis Club at the corner of 12th [now Minor Ave.] and Madison Streets...The crowd, was of the right sort, and the number of pretty girls in summer costume did much to stimulate the spirit with which the matches were played."

This was the fifth year that the club had been producing these grand summer matches on their clay courts behind the Martin Van Buren Stacy mansion on Madison. But this year, 1895, was the first that those "pretty girls in summer costumes" took to the courts themselves and perspired in their own singles and doubles matches.

The historical photo of a woman's doubles play is one of two tournament scenes recently uncovered by a local collector in a First Hill family album. The other photo is captioned, "July 1895." No doubt, both were taken during the Olympic Club's summer event.

This is an action shot. The women on the right wait to receive the ball from the woman in white on the left who is near the top of her serve. If this is the

women's doubles championship match, then the winners Miss Anderson and Miss Keown of Tacoma will defeat Miss Riley and Miss Gazzam of Seattle, and win for their efforts a pair of silver scissors with a thimble in a case and a cut-glass, silver mounted ink stand.

The following year, 1896, the Olympic Club changed its name to the Seattle Tennis Club. In 1903 the crowded club built additional courts up Madison Street at Summit Ave., and in 1919

migrated much further up Madison to their new and present home on the shores of Lake Washington.

The Martin Van Buren Stacy mansion, of course, stayed behind and still stays put at the northeast corner of Madison and Boren. It is one of the very few remaining remnants of the old, elegant, and well-appointed wealth that was once First Hill society.

For 84 years it has been the home of the University (Men's) Club, another remnant of matriculated class, which in 1930 a Seattle Times writer characterized like this: "If you are a member of the

University Club, you are suspected of certain things—of being a good bridge player, an excellent host, an interesting sort of person, a man of position and substance and achievement. And many men who pay dues to every organization in or near town refer to it as 'the club,' which, after all, is the whole story."

Right A somewhat later view of the University Club after the large Madison St. addition. *Bottom* this pan from the Coppin's watertower looks to the northeast and shows over the onion-domed Carkeek mansion at Madison St. and Boren Ave. both the Stacy mansion (University club) and the Tennis grounds which is also marked with an arrow.

27 The Kalmar Hotel

In 1962 when Seattle showed the world Century 21, a fair with "forward thrust," University of Washington architect Victor Steinbrueck first published his sketchbook (now a local classic), *Seattle Cityscape*.

One of its most lovingly rendered pen-&-ink drawings was of the Hotel Kalmar. Steinbrueck's own caption for his sketch reads, in part: "The only remaining (Seattle) example of an early pioneer hotel is the old Kalmar Hotel at Sixth Avenue and James Street...With its pumpkin-colored wooden siding and band-sawn details, it has been a picturesque part of Seattle's personality. Built in 1881...much of Seattle's history has been viewed from its wide veranda, but now it is being destroyed to make room for the freeway."

Steinbrueck's sketches were published in May of 1962. One month earlier, the *Seattle Times* reported, that the Kalmar was razed in a "rumble of wrecker's derricks and clamshell loaders."

For more than 70 years the Kalmar had lived intimately next to a different rumble, one that was regular—the clanging struggle of the James St. cable cars as they gripped their way up and down the steep side of First Hill. Leonard Brand, who with his sister Viola were the last managers and residents of the Kalmar, was positively fond of that noise. "That clang and clatter didn't bother me at all. Now and again, though, and very often in the middle of the night, they'd shut down the line for repairs. The quiet would wake me right out of a deep sleep."

Actually, he'd never known anything else. The cable cars had rocked the baby Leonard to sleep, for he was only 3 months old when his parents bought and moved into the Michigan House and renamed it after his mother's hometown in Sweden.

This scene was probably photographed for the Brands who are posing on the veranda. Leonard is in his mother's arms and Viola stands by. The Kalmar was the only home these children knew until they were forced by the freeway to retire to West Seattle.

The Kalmar was a workingman's hotel—when there was work. Many were Scandinavian loggers attracted, no doubt, by the name. They were ordinarily sober bachelors who spent their money not on skid road but sent it home. The Kalmar was their home away from home.

One young guest first signed the register in 1912 and stayed until 1957 when, sadly, he was moved to a rest home.

Two years earlier, in 1955, the Kalmar's fate was prescribed when the path of the proposed, what was then called "Seattle tollway," was drawn through it. Since the freeway, that grandest materialization of progress, could not be moved, local preservationists tried to freeze the Kalmar, promoting a city-wide policy that would prevent the "removal, alteration or remodeling of historical properties without the city council's approval."

Courtesy of Lawton Gowey

Top The Kalmar in its last days. *Above* Victor Steinbrueck's loving sketch.

In 1960, responding in the *Seattle Times* to the imminent destruction of the Kalmar and three other historical landmarks by the freeway, Steinbrueck reflected, "To let them be destroyed is esthetic idiocy on the part of the city. It would be like the case of an idiot who lives only in the present and has no memory of the past...Things which have associations and give us a sense of memory are part of our city."

Steinbrueck lamented in the same *Times* article, "When I go back now to many of these places, nothing is left...I have only my pictures." Of course, both the attempts to freeze and later to move the Kalmar failed. And now we too are left with only the pictures.

Courtesy of Seattle Engineering Dept.

28   Madison Beach Bathing

The older view of the Madison Park swimming beach was photographed during the first year of the Great Depression and the last day of a regional heat wave. On Wednesday, August 14, 1930, the thermometer reached a high of 85 degrees. There were out-of-control fires burning in the Cascades and out-of-work men and women cooling off in Lake Washington.

And there were kids too. Those who could pass the dog paddle test were allowed to venture past the ropes to the crowded diving dock and its 20-foot tower, (which at this moment does not appear to be too popular).

The contemporary hot scene was shot on the Sunday afternoon of July 15, 1985. That day also hit a high of 85, but here the beach users are not so inclined to cool off. The intervening 54 years have seen swimming beach behavior stay more-and-more out of the water and on the beach where the bodies are liberally exposed to the sun and each other. (In order to shoot across this second sea of sunbathing bodies, the "now" scene was photographed from about 50 yards south of the "then.")

In 1930 women were no longer wearing dresses into the water, but men were not yet wearing trunks. The result was a kind of unisex swimming suit which made for a very poor tan line. In fact, tanning was then still thought to be a rather rude evidence of having to work out of doors and not of choosing to leisurely languish in the sun.

There is no grass lawn in the historical scene, just a sandy path and a long line of wood benches. The sloping lawn that allows today's narcissists to lie down together in herds like sunning sea lions was landscaped in the late 1930s by out-of-work depression time WPA labor wearing bib-overalls not bikinis.

The ferry steaming off to Kirkland from its Madison St. slip is the 160-ft-long steel-hulled *Lincoln*. The run took 17 minutes and there was a popular coffee shop on board. For 25 years the *Lincoln* was the mainstay of this trans-lake run, until 1940 when the *Leschi* was

76

moved over from its Leschi-Bellevue run after the opening of the Mercer Island bridge.

The *Lincoln* was built in 1914 at Houghton's Lake Washington shipyards, and during the early 1940s she regularly returned there as the commuter vessel for wartime shipyard workers.

In 1948 the *Lincoln* was moved to the Fauntleroy-Vashon Island run. Auto-mobile ferry service to Kirkland from Madison Park, the last on the lake, ended on August 31, 1950, a little over a year after tolls were lifted from the Mercer Island bridge.

Top An early century scene along the Madison Park waterfront. This view was photographed before the lake was lowered 9 ft in 1916. Of this scene only the Pioneer's hall on the far left remains today. *Middle* An early 1890s view of the same stretch of beachfront. *Bottom* One of the trackless trolleys that replaced the Madison St. Cable Railway. The ferry at the Madison St. dock is the Lincoln.

29 Poplars on Madison Street

These "now" and "then" views look east up Madison St. from Sixth Ave. They share only one detail, the backside, or west wall, of the Sorrento Hotel. It is not the centerpiece of either scene, but can be detected in the historical photograph as the faint gray structure a few blocks up Madison.

The oldest scene dates from 1910 or 11. Then, the First Hill stretch of Madison St., from Sixth Ave. to Broadway, was a fashionable strip of brick apartments and hotels standing side by side (and often replacing) the old First Hill mansions of the city's elite. (The Carkeeks, Burkes, Stimsons and Fryes all lived on Madison.) In 1910 the Sorrento was the newest addition.

This street was also lined by what Sophie Frye Bass described in her book *Pig-Tail Days In Old Seattle*, as "the pride of Madison Street...the stately poplar trees made it the most attractive place

in town." The fast-growing poplars were donated by "many public spirited women," but did not survive into the 1930s when Bass wrote her book. By then, she lamented, they had "given way protestingly to business."

In the early 1960s this block between Sixth and Seventh avenues gave way to the freeway—despite the protests. Another still lamented loss occurred here 20 years earlier, in 1940, when the Madison St. cable cars gave way to gas-powered buses.

The two cable cars in the older scene are vintage stock of the Madison St. Cable Railway. They were brought here in 1890 when the line first opened service through the forest to Lake Washington. (These cars, numbers 34 and 38 were scrapped in 1912.)

The Madison cable cars were notorious for the amount of advertising hung inside and out. The white sign on the front of car #38—in the foreground—reads, "White City, Madison Park, Cool Place, Refreshments, Amusements." White City was a short-lived promotion by the Seattle Electric Company, the cable railway's owners, designed to attract riders out to Madison Park.

It was not a new idea. From its 1890 beginning, Madison Park was a trolley park, whose amusements were meant to encourage fares and suburban settlement. White City's carnival-type rides were the last of these planned attractions, opening in 1910 and closing in 1912.

By then the top attraction at the lake end of Madison St. was not the park but the ferry-slip and the ferryboat named after the 16th president of the United States, Lincoln. (See previous story)

Madison St. was named for the union's fifth president. Pioneer Arthur Denny, while platting Seattle's streets in alliterative pairs, named the street one block south of Madison, Marion, after a younger brother, James Marion Denny. Arthur needed another M.

Courtesy of Lawton Gowey

Courtesy of Lawton Gowey

Top The same scene east of Sixth Ave. sans poplars and a short time before the I-5 freeway razed the block. *Middle* after the freeway but still showing the old First Presbyterian Church at 7th Ave. *Bottom* A part of White City.

Courtesy of Old Seattle Paperworks, Pike Place Market

30 Garden in the Sky

When it was built in 1899 the Lincoln was the city's most elegant hotel. Nine stories high, it was also a landmark taller than the buildings down around Pioneer Square and taller than those along the city's growing commercial strip, Second Ave. And the hotel's elevated setting at Fourth and Madison made it seem more monumental still. Constructed of white brick and stone, the Lincoln glowed as it reflected the setting sun.

The historical view was photographed from the top of the hotel. The vine-snarled trellises of the Lincoln's well-groomed roof garden could be alluringly glimpsed from the street, but the garden itself was most commonly

enjoyed not at first-hand by those on the hotel's register, but through the many hand-painted postcards of it for sale in the lobby. (They are still a familiar item to local postcard collectors.)

This view looks southeast towards the top-heavy cupola of the county's courthouse (upper-right) on First Hill. There on the courthouse roof is a clue which dates this photo. Barely visible through the haze is a giant welcome sign, set there in 1908 for the Puget Sound visit of Teddy Roosevelt's Great White Fleet.

The other closer and more classical dome sits atop the United Methodist church at Sixth and Marion—and still does. In 1908 the sanctuary was under construction; the congregation worshiped

Courtesy of University of Washington Historical Photography Collection

United Methodist Church

in the basement. (Now this landmark which gives some architectural soul to a neighborhood of skyscrapers sits on some very material real estate. A part of the congregation wishes to put another skyscraper in its place.) The city's Land-mark Preservation Board disagrees.

When it opened in 1900 the Lincoln was Seattle's first apartment-hotel. The plan did not work. What gave it promi-nence on the city's skyline, also put it too far away from the city's commercial district. The Lincoln was soon converted into a straight commercial hotel, but faltered in this role as well.

The business then passed through a number of different managers and owners. The last of these was the Madison Realty Company which bought the hotel on November 1, 1919 and proceeded to sink $75,000 into remodeling it and its main floor businesses. Included were a restau-rant, a cigar and candy store, a tailor shop, a drug store, a millinery shop and

The Lincoln Hotel Fire of April, 1920

Courtesy of Seattle Public Library

a beauty salon.

On the morning of April 7, 1920 in the first hour after midnight, Mrs. C. A. Gross proprietor of the cigar store and Mrs. T. Waters owner of the beauty shop met for a moment in the hotel lobby before leaving for home. Their chat was quickly concluded when a "thinly clad" man rushed by them crying, "Fire."

Within the hour the firetrap

Lincoln—it was brick on the outside only and wooden within—was a roaring furnace. The hotel was lost, including three of its guests and one fireman. But more than 300 were saved; many of them heroically slid down ropes and ladders. The "tons of water" dumped on the fire created a river down Madison St. and Third Ave. It was the last watering for the Lincoln's roof garden.

Madison W from 4th
Feb 23 07 SPo

31 The Mess on Madison

I t is the street here which is the photographer's real subject.

This 1907 view looks down Madison from Fourth Ave. and a banner is stretched across the street at midblock. It warns, "All persons are prohibited from walking on street car tracks." Evidently, this does not include the worker standing on the center rail of the Madison St. cable's uphill track. It was through the slit in that center rail that the cable cars attached to the continuously running cable. With the street's regrading the entire cable system was brought above ground, and its mysteries revealed to the curiosity of "sidewalk superintendents" and riders alike.

This inspecting could be dangerous.

Throughout the regrading years the local press was scattered with stories of persons falling from cars and tracks, of embarrassing descents into the mud, and an occasional loss of limb. It was also a losing proposition for many of the businesses along the way. Not only were they assessed for these "improvements," but added to this financial injury was the dirty and difficult detouring required of customers to reach front doors. Some businesses organized to speed up the projects, while others tried to stop them. In this, obviously, they worked against each other.

For 16 years, the Third Avenue Theater, the frame structure with the tower seen just right of center, operated with more than average success as one of the most popular playhouses in America. Here because of the regrading along 3rd Ave. and Madison St., it is recently closed. One month after this photograph was taken, it was torn down.

The Lincoln Hotel's Madison St. entrance, on the right of our image is about to be abandoned as the street and sidewalk are chipped away. With the eight to ten foot lowering of both Madison St. and Fourth Ave., the Lincoln would gain a daylight story. Then the elegant entrance seen in our view became a second-story arch above the new doorway. That passage admitted patrons for 13 more years until the still well-remembered Lincoln Hotel fire of April 7, 1920 "regraded" all. (There's more on that disaster in the preceding story.)

The tower at the foot of Madison St. is part of the fire station on the waterfront. The drying tower of today's waterfront fire station can also be seen in the contemporary view down Madison from Fourth Ave. Like everything else on the waterfront, it hides behind the gray interruption of the Alaska Way Viaduct.

Our primary historical image is dated Saturday, February 23, 1907. Frederick & Nelson's rooftop sign is seen in the center of our view, then at the northwest corner of Second Ave. and Madison. An advertisement in the Friday *Times* reported that "the department store under one roof with everything to furnish the home complete" was having a "Saturday Special." Featured were: "Golden Oak Parlor Stands for one dollar; Zinc Washboards for 30 cents; and Decorated Cup and Saucer Sets for 17 cents." It was, of course, "cash only, and all sales final."

The February 23, Saturday *Times* reported that Mark Twain had just purchased a new dress suit of all white broadcloth "as immaculate as the new fallen snow"; that "six beautiful bay view lots on Magnolia Bluff could be had, together, for $1500"; and that "a Professor Matteucio of the Vesuvius Observatory was of the opinion that all life would be destroyed in late March if and when the earth's atmosphere is ignited by a collision with the tail of a newly discovered comet heading this way."

However, the most sensational Saturday news was reported in the Sunday *Times*. Its banner headline read "MAN'S HEAD FOUND ON ROOF." The story explained that what horrified linemen had discovered in a tin pail on the roof of

Courtesy of Lawton Gowey

the Oriental Building was "only" part of a cadaver left there to cool by medical students.

The Oriental roof was on Second Ave. near Cherry St. A second Saturday sensation from an upper story occurred one block away, when a young woman jumped from the second floor of the Paxton Hotel at Third Ave. and Cherry St. The *Times* reported that "she ran wildly up and down the street dressed only in her night clothes." Later, she claimed to have been sleepwalking, but the *Times* reporter concluded "that she had imbibed a bit too freely of the glass that gladdens." This wild performance had excited the sell-out crowd on its way to the Grand Opera House to see the "burned-cork artists" from Seattle High School perform their very popular annual minstrel show.

The Grand Opera House was on the east side of Cherry St. between Second Ave., the site of the Oriental Building, and Third Ave., the site of the Paxton Hotel. The back of the Opera House can be seen in our second historical photo-graph. Just beyond it is the Alaska Building. Both structures are still stand-ing; however, the theater has been

Courtesy of University of Washington Historical Photography Collection

changed some into the Cherry St. garage.

In the foreground, the centerpiece of this photograph, the James St. cable car No. 71 poses at the intersection with Third Ave. Like the line on Madison St., the regrading here has made the trip up First Hill an elevating but dangerous adventure.

In the Madison St. comparison between the "now" and "then," every-thing has changed. The building on the left is the last Olympic National Bank which was razed by implosion in 1983. In February 1907, it was called the Empire Building and was still under con-struction.

The ships on Elliott Bay seemed to have paused through the duration of the Fourth Ave. regrade.

32   The Grand Emporium

The historical scene looks across Second Ave. and Madison St. toward Seattle's first grand emporium during or some little time after 1906. That was the year that D. E. Frederick and Nels Nelson, after moving their partnership through four locations in sixteen years, could at last stretch their name the length of an entire city block—the Rialto Block.

Frederick and Nelson opened a second-hand store in 1890, but finding it easier to buy unused merchandise than ferret out old, they dropped the nearly new and somehow learned the marketing skills to become, in time, the "largest and finest department store west of the Mississippi and north of San Francisco."

In 1897 in the first flush of the Klondike gold rush, they moved into the two center storefronts of the then new Rialto Building, and in 1906 bought out the block.

Soon shopping at Frederick & Nel-

5/26/08

Courtesy of Michael Maslan

Courtesy of Old Seattle Paperworks, Pike Place Market

Top Frederick & Nelson's Rialto Block all decked out for the 1908 visit of the Great White Fleet. (See Story #19 for more on that occasion.)*Above,* The Rialto Black some little time after F-&-N vacatged it for the store's present location at 5th and Pine.

son was an experience quite the opposite of the often mad rush through the crass conveniences of one of today's giant dis- count warehouses. At Fredericks you were invited to take classes, visit an art gal- lery, or klatsch with friends over tea, or just ride the sublimely smooth hydraulic elevator. The big center room with the high ceiling for hanging tapestries and Persian rugs was a kind of sanctuary for consumption. Years later, you may not remember what you bought there, but you would recall its luxurious "aura."

This touch of class was also found in the elaborately decorated show win- dows along Second Ave., and even in the street itself, where every morning the store's delivery service of 16 heavy teams of horses paraded down the length of Second Ave. enroute from the stables.

Nels Nelson died in 1906, but D. E. Frederick, or Fred as his friends called him, continued to make the right moves including the one in 1918 that took him "out of town" all the way north to F & N's present location at 5th and Pine.

In 1929 D. E. Frederick retired to his home in the Highlands and soon sold his grand emporium to what he called his "model," the even grander Marshall Field & Co. of Chicago.

Twenty years later, after Frederick had also ultimately moved on, his old golfing cronie, 95-year-old Chamber of Commerce publicist and *Seattle Times* columnist, C. T. Conover, recalled that "Fred started from scratch and built a business known from coast to coast and one of the great Puget Sound fortunes." Warming up, Conover characterized Frederick as a kind of heroic capitalist saint who "left a record of straight shooting, fair play, honorable dealing, enlightened vision, common sense, civic enterprise, public spirit, and generous support for every worthy cause."

THE GROWTH OF THE BON MARCHE

Twelve years ago last May an unpretentious Notion Store began business at the corner of Cedar Street and First Avenue, then known as Front Street. It was an ordinary little store—thirty feet wide.

The founder was Edward L. Nordhoff, of Chicago, who with his wife Josephine had decided to venture their all—a few hundred dollars only—in this out-of-the-way retail store. The firm was termed The Bon Marche, Nordhoff & Co. From the start, however, a difference existed between this mercantile venture and the usual small store. The founder was a man of rare business sagacity—one who believed in MAKING business and not waiting for business to come to him.

And so it was not long before the little notion shop began to be talked of. the business increased and soon, too, additional floor space was taken by annexing the adjoining room. In still another year this first store of The Bon Marche was changed for the double front building. The latter store was on the opposite corner of First Avenue and Cedar Street from the original business place.

The brick building of the last named store was built to accommodate The Bon Marche's needs.

By this time—1894—the firm was returning street car fare to customers from South Seattle and The Bon Marche was steadily gaining in size also and popularity.

In October, 1896, the business was moved to Second Avenue, near Pike Street—part of the present location—with a frontage of 60 feet on Second avenue. The entire stock by this time aggregated $50,000 instead of the few hundreds of the original start.

In May, 1897, the store enlarged to include frontage on Pike Street. The next change, in May, 1898, absorbed 60 feet more on Second Avenue.

In the spring of 1899 Mr. Nordhoff died and his widow continued the business with the active aid of Rudolph Nordhoff, of Buffalo, New York, a brother of the deceased.

The final enlargement of ground floor space of The Bon Marche was made June 1, 1901, when the corner at Pike Street and Second Avenue became a part of the store.

In less than thirty days from the above date it became apparent that the entire first floor and basement of this enlarged store were too small to accommodate the business, and immediate plans were made to build a new and commodious store. The story of the rebuilding of The Bon Marche has been a subject of interest the past half year to nearly every person in Seattle and vicinity.

These simple facts, therefore, as to the new store which was formally opened this week with the largest crowds from Seattle and surrounding towns ever gathered under one roof in Seattle.

The frontage is 180 feet on Second Avenue and 110 feet on Pike Street.

Three stories and a commodious basement give, at present, ample space for our needs—making 91,000 square feet of selling and storeroom space.

All but the third floor are devoted to salesrooms.

The third floor is a stock room and contains, also, the business offices.

It is, all in all, the best appointed department store in the West.

It is the well started foundation for the largest retail business west of Chicago, and, mayhap, west of New York.

THE BON MARCHE—NOVEMBER 1902—OPENING WEEK

The Bon Marche

Nordhoff & Co.   The Big Store

1419 to 1435 Second Ave.   SEATTLE   115 to 123 Pike St.

We fill Mail Orders for out-of-town Customers promptly.

Our mail order department is in charge of a competent woman of years of experience in mail order work.

Send for our Christmas Catalogue of Holiday Goods

A *Splendid* Price-List, well illustrated with the Goods you need.

33   The Launching of the *Fortuna*

Jim Faber, left, and Captain Bob Matson, right, two of Seattle's most familiar "old salts" pose in the contemporary photo while they inspect Faber's new book, *Steamer's Wake*. They have opened it to pages 220 and 221 where this story's historical photo of the 1906 launching of the Lake Washington steamer *Fortuna* is given a generous two-page spread.

Faber and Matson stand beside Lake Washington Blvd., a short ways south of Leschi Park and near the site where Captain John Anderson built his trim steamer. The siting is close but approximate. In 1906 this shoreline was still undeveloped, the lake nine feet higher, and no boulevard ran by here.

And there are other "relative" connections between the "now" and "then" photos. Captain Matson is Captain Anderson's nephew. In the historical photo the older captain stands on the right side of the ceremonial stand below the *Fortuna*'s bow.

In 1932 the uncle put his nephew to work. After a scholarly day at Garfield High, the 17-year-old Matson hiked down to his uncle's Leschi Park waterfront office for four hours of work aboard another of the captain's small lake steamers, the *Dawn*. His depression time pay was a good dollar a day for four hours work.

In his time the young deckhand became a mate, a purser, and a skipper who worked the last of the Lake Washington steamers including the carferries *Lincoln* and *Leschi*. Captain Matson was in the pilot house when the *Leschi* made the last run between Madison Park and Kirkland on August 31, 1950. Matson also spent time skippering the region's most famous ferry, the streamlined *Kalakala*.

When Uncle John gave his nephew a job on the lake he'd already been working it for more than 40 years. Born in 1868 in Gottenburg Sweden the son of a seafaring man, the young John dropped his studies and went to sea, crossing the Atlantic at the age of 14. Working his way west on the Canadian Pacific R.R., he ultimately settled here. While still in his early 20s, the captain began to build his steamboat armada on the lake behind Seattle.

Anderson's boats were the classics of Lake Washington's mosquito fleet, and many of them were given euphonious and antique names like the *Ramona*, *Urania*, *Xanthus*, *Cyrene*, *Atlanta*, *Triton*, *Aquilo*, *Calipso* and in 1906 his pride, the *Fortuna*.

In *Steamer's Wake*, Jim Faber described the launching of the trim steamer *Fortuna* as "the high water mark in the fortunes of Seattle's lake steamers." The actual launching had its shallower side. Soon after the *Fortuna* started her slide to the water, the wooden slab supports collapsed leaving her stern in the water but her bow in the mud.

Although not damaged, it took a few frustrating hours to pull her free.

And the short ceremony that preceded the launch was also dampened with laughter when the first wake this steamer threw was alcoholic. The *Seattle Times* remarked that after the 13-year-old Miss Daisy Johnson (waiting beneath her white bonnet beside Captain Anderson) "peformed her task in the most creditable manner" of breaking the bottle of champagne against the bow and crying with a clear voice "I christen thee *Fortuna*," immediately "several urchins, not one over 15 years of age...began licking up the precious fluid, running their tongues up the side of the steamer...The spectacle threw the attending crowd into convulsions."

Besides this scene of the *Fortuna* and its waiting urchins, Jim Faber's *Steamer's Wake* includes 250 more wonderfully displayed and wittily captioned "Mosquito Fleet" photos. Faber worked on the book for three years. It was worth our wait.

Courtesy of Capt. Bob Matson

The *Fortuna* soon after her launch but temporarily stuck in her ways.

34   Along the Bike Path

For a few exhilarating years around the turn of the century, bike riding was a popular craze in Seattle, and the building of bike trails around its hills an ingenious engineering trick. Those were the early pre-gear years of bicycling.

When a writer for *Sports Afield* visited this city in 1897 and tested the new bike trail to Lake Washington, the weekly *Argus* repeated for the locals the sophisticate's belief that "had the old Roman road builders dropped into Seattle this spring, they would have been heartily surprised and doffed their hats to the wheelmen who can lead a six-foot path through virgin forests, in and out of a terrible rough country, along the sides of exceedingly steep hills. When completed, the grades will be few and all easy for even a novice to ride."

Here is, perhaps, one of those novices on a part of that path. And the photo does a good job of showing both the easy grade and that "terrible rough country." Its distant view also reveals

why the Argus editor dared to draw a moral from the national arbiter's remarks. "I do not care who the critic is or how many wonderful sights he had seen...he cannot pass over the Lake Washington path...without being impressed with the magnificent panorama revealed at every turn on this snake-like path."

But which turn in the snake is this? As often as I have seen this popular photograph in exhibits and publications none of them, including the excellent short history *Bicycling in Seattle, 1897-1904* by Seattle's bicycle authority Frank Cameron, has pinned it down. So I first went searching for Frank Cameron and a caption for this photo more precise than the usual generality "along the bike path." And I found that the one-time master mechanic for Bucky's bike delivery service (see story #92 in *Seattle Now and Then*) was now (in 1986) "repairing" or moving humans with his new duties at Traveler's Aid.

Frank and I put our heads together, switched a few gears and soon determined that this view rather quickly gives itself away. As surely as a fingerprint, the profile of the horizon and the shape of the shoreline identifies the first land across the water as Mercer Island. And more precisely, Mercer Island as seen from what was then called Leschi Heights.

So this is near the Leschi Park end of the Lake Washington Bike Trail and more than ten wild but relatively level cinder-surfaced snaking miles out from the city center. Frank also remembered from his research that it was here that the cyclists who did not turn around faced a fork in the road, and both ways were steep. The one descended to the amusements at Leschi Park and the other to the top of Leschi Heights. The trail's split at the photo's lower left corner may be that fork.

Much of the old and short-lived bicycle path was eventually transformed into city streets—most notably the scenic Interlaken Blvd. that still winds through the woods at the north end of Capitol Hill.

And where in the "now" is this scene? The most likely conversion is the curve where E. Terrace St. bends slightly to the southeast before it circles north and turns into 36th Ave. The historical scene also looks to the southeast, and both the "now" and "then" are near the top of the ridge above Leschi Park but not at it. I'll boldly say that had the woman biker held her pose for 85 years,

Courtesy of University of Washington Historical Photography Collection

she could have overheard the endearments of the strolling family in the contemporary scene.

That's the John and Karen McCoy family who have since this photo was taken added a second boy, Luke, to Aaron and Zena. Karen, who was a nurse at Harborview Hospital, and John, who was the religion editor at the P.I., lived near this scene until the summer of 1986. Then the family left to train for jobs in Lima, Peru where John will be writing for the Latin American News under the sponsorship of the Maryknoll Missions.

The *Argus* editor, concluded that this was a "wheelman's paradise" where "lost in the forest...among the birds that spring from twig to twig...he drinks in pure air and thanks God for the power which enables him to appreciate nature." Frank Cameron adds that in 1901 warnings were issued on Capitol Hill about bears frightening bicyclists on the Lake Washington Bike Path.

Boat Landing, Leschi Park, Seattle, Washington

35 Retouching Leschi

A few years back while thumbing through some photos at the Oregon Historical Society, I first discovered this very inviting and decidedly idealized scene. (Although I have already published this scene in the notes section of my first collection of these Seattle "Now and Then"s, it's here again because it deserves to be.) This photograph has been made downright sweet by an artist's creation of some cumulus clouds that resemble cotton candy.

At the bottom of the photo the retouch-artist continued his work enveloping the heads of two women in the fog that surrounds the picture's caption, "1061 Boat Landing, Leschi Park..." I made a photocopy of the artist-photographer's work, laying it on a tilting table next to a window, but using a steady tripod, I got a good negative.

The next time I stumbled upon this scene was in Wade Vaughn's book *Seattle-Leschi Diary*. Wade copied his view from a postcard. There are no confectionary

Genevieve McCoy

92

clouds and the women have their heads. Instead, the postcard's caption has been decapitated. Vaughn ex-plains below his use of this view that once a caption did - exist, and that it dated the scene 1911 and added this stock postcardish description: "Leschi Park is a small picturesque Park bordering Lake Washington at Yesler Way, and is a favorite starting point for excursionists over the beautiful lake."

Actually, the old Leschi was much more than picturesque. As the dappled light in this photo suggests, in its day Leschi was a resort of fair weather pleasures where the differences between indoors and out, sun and shade, and land and lake were creatively confused by long verandas, arboreal promenades, gazebos, bandstands, ornamental gables and arches.

The Leschi boathouse was a wonderful harbor built beneath eight gables and a decorated tower that covered, but did not hide, rows of wood canoes when they, not motorcars, were the principal means of transport for romance. Here you see only the boathouse sign, far right, on the dock which leads out to the covered canoes.

Nor do you see the Leschi Pavilion, although the photo was taken from its veranda. The pavilion was immense, extending far out over the water, to the right, and far into the park, to the left. The scene of many dances, romances, and stage shows, its single most famous attraction was the 1906 performance by the "divine" Sarah Bernhardt.

What is in this picture is Captain John Anderson's landing for his lake excursion launches. Just beyond his depot, and poking its second story above the Anderson sign, is the Lake Washington Hotel and Restaurant. It was built in 1890, or less than two years after an historic event that turned "Fleaburg" (this spot's popular name in the 1880s) into Leschi.

The Lake Washington Cable Railway's formal opening was on September 28, 1888. It took 16 minutes for its open cars to run the three-plus roller-coaster miles out Yelser Way from Pioneer Square—a fact that encouraged many businessmen to build homes on the hill behind the park. The cable railway's power house is half-hidden behind the trees on the photo's left. We can see the smokestacks.

In 1913, or only two years after this scene was shot, the Leschi auto ferry began its 27 years of steaming between here and Bellevue. The July 2, 1940

Above Leschi Park quiet in the sping-time sun of April 4, 1899 with the clearcut Leschi Heights behind.

Courtesy of University of Washington Historical Photography Collection

opening of the Lake Washington Floating Bridge put a sudden end to that. Only five weeks later on August 10, the last cable car to run out Yesler completed 52 years of a service many now wish was still running.

Actually, the end of this old Leschi scene was over many years earlier. I chose a symbolic 1925 when the oiled-gravel surface of Lakeside Ave. was cut down through the center of our photograph. After that it was perhaps unlikely that any artist-photographer of this view would be inspired to add edible clouds.

Courtesy of Washington State Historical Society

36 The Life of Fortson Square

The original platting of Seattle left some pleasing irregularities along Mill St., now Yesler Way. In 1852 pioneers Doc Maynard and Arthur Denny could not agree on how their streets should meet. The results were anomalies like the small triangular block we see across Yesler Way in both our "now" and "then." At the turn of the century it was named "Fortson Square" after a Seattle captain who participated in the Philippines war. Its more popular name was Pigeon Square.

Second Ave. ran to two sides of this triangular "square." On the left is Maynard's original line. It parallels the buildings. But on the right is another Second Ave.—the one bent to meet up with Denny's version to the north (the photographer's side) of Yesler Way.

The photographer was Ashael Curtis, and he recorded this scene in 1911, sometime during the baseball season. On the back of the Yesler cable car (lower right) is a sign which reads, "Northwestern League Base Ball Today, take this car." Little Dugdale Park, the "Post Stamp Park," was at 12th Ave. and Yesler Way. There's no telling if the suited males hanging from the sides of the cable car are following the sign's advice. In 1911 men wore suits everywhere. (Most of that season, the Seattle Turks were in a cellar race with Victoria. Spokane was in first place.)

As this view reveals, the south side of Skid Road (Yesler Way) was a melting pot of early-century Americana. Pictured in this block are: an Italian grocery, a Greek restaurant, the Paradise; two big bars, two hotels, a shoe shop, barber shop, and hand laundry. All of this was in a mix with Seattle's first Chinatown. Here also are the Peking Cafe, the Hee Wo Chinese Medicine Co., the King Chong tailors, and the Chinese Import-

The difference half-a-year can make—during the 1928 Second Ave. extension.

ers. And everything is topped with gaudy signage.

In 1911 Pigeon Square was itself an inviting scene. Outfitted with benches and an ornate U.S. Weather Bureau exhibit with glass-enclosed barometers and thermometers (seen just above the cable car), it was a place to hang out or wait for the Grant St. electric trolleys that ran south from here to Georgetown.

Now no busses stop here, and neither pigeons nor people sit in the bushes which have taken the place of the benches.

In 1928 this neighborhood was cut in half when the elbow in the arm of the old Second Ave. was straightened in the Second Ave. extension. The civic interest was to connect the railroad stations to the foot of Jackson St. with hotels and retailers north of Yesler Way. However, "Seattle's Market Street" didn't do much for business south of Yesler Way. The one-two punch of the extension and the 1929 crash sent this skid road neighborhood into a lengthy decline.

Courtesy of Seattle Engineering Dept.

Confluence of Black and White Rivers.

"There's not in this wide world
 a valley so sweet
"As the vale in whose bosom
 the bright waters meet"
 Moore

37 "Where the Bright Waters Meet"

*There's not in this wide world
A valley so sweet
As the vale in whose bosom
The bright waters meet.*

So Carrie Coe jotted this oft-quoted verse beneath the original print of this river scene. The poetry was not hers but the photo was, and judging from the other photos in her album, she took it sometime in the early 1890s. Although the years have physically dimmed it, this photograph is still a peculiarly bright record; it's probably the only surviving photo of natives on a river that is no more.

Fortunately, Carrie Coe also tells us which "waters meet" here in this "valley so sweet." Above her photo is another caption. It reads,"confluence of Black and White Rivers." We might have guessed it.

For many years that confluence was the first fork in the Duwamish River upstream from Elliott Bay. For someone polling or paddling up the Duwamish in a scow or dugout, it was the turnoff for

The native scene *below* was also photographed by Carrie Coe and was part of the collection that included the "confluence" scene, and so may be also of the Black or White rivers.

Lake Washington. If you turned left you entered the Black; if right, the White (since renamed the Green). It was this confluence of the two that formed the Duwamish.

In Coe's photo we can't say for sure which is the Black and which the White. If you sense, as I do, that the dugout canoes are riding, not fighting, the current, then that is the Black in the foreground in its last moments before it joins the White beyond to become the Duwamish on the right.

Carrie Coe moved to Seattle with her doctor husband Franz Coe in 1888—or about 6,000 years after Mt. Tahoma (Rainier) blew its top and dropped part of it on Tukwila and Renton. Before that unloading, Lake Washington was part of Puget Sound. After the eruption, the slow-forming Black River was the way the lake eventually reunited itself with the Sound.

It was a natural habit that each year the spring floods that gorged the White River would push the waters of the Black back into the lake. Thus, the natives called it Mox La Push, or "two mouths." The settlers called it the Black River because it was often silted with the remnants of the mountain's cap and ice age droppings. Judging from her description of "bright waters," Carrie Coe couldn't have been touring the Black River during the spring.

We don't know how Coe and her camera got up the river, but they might have taken the train. As early as 1877 coaches and coal gondolas followed the river's edge on a narrow-gauged track built between Seattle and the coal fields of Renton. In 1883 the Northern Pacific built a connection between this Black River Junction and Stuck Junction a few miles south. This, at last, gave Seattle a train connection with Tacoma and thereby with the rest of the country.

By 1909 when the Milwaukee Road came through here, there were five railroad lines crossing this Black River Junction. That amounted to as many as 40 passenger trains a day, in addition to the freights. Times have changed.

The contemporary photo looks west from the bridge of the Milwaukee Road's branch line to Tacoma at what remains of the Black River. We are a few hundred yards upstream from the Duwamish where there is no longer any confluence of "bright waters." In 1916 when Lake Washington was lowered nine feet for the

Another Carrie Coe photo. *Below* hop-picking natives in the White (now Green) River valley.

new government ship canal at Shilshole Bay, the Black River's headwaters were dried up. Since then the Black has been bulldozed, black-topped and, this last part of it, trenched into a drainage ditch.

But the valley Carrie Coe sang about is still "so sweet." The Duwamish greenbelt that runs south from Riverton past the Black River Junction and through Tukwila is still picturesque until it spreads out into the parking lots and warehouses of Southcenter.

38 The Lost River

I first uncovered this romantic river scene in a *Post Intelligencer* photo-feature titled "Canoeing From Lake To Sound." Originally published on Sunday, September 9, 1906, it featured 12 illustrations of a relaxed flotilla making its way down the old river route from Lake Washington to Puget Sound.

The original story was confined to one page, and so the pictures were both small and grainy. Although I wished to see this scene more clearly—a common desire with old news photos—I knew that my chances of ever finding an original print, or even negative, were very slim. Recently, those odds were suddenly "fattened" when a friend, John Hanawalt of the Old Seattle Paperworks in the Pike Place Market, showed me a stack of old photographs he had uncovered, and flipped to an original print of this Black River scene.

This is a truly lost place. The Black River used to run out of the southern end of Lake Washington enroute to its union with the Duwamish River and Elliott Bay. But before it coursed a mile, it was joined by the Cedar River at a confluence which was just a few yards north of what is now the Renton intersection of Rainier Ave. and Airport Way. The contemporary photograph shows the view north through that intersection.

The old *Post Intelligencer*'s caption for this photograph reads, "Black River, near Cedar River." If the boaters were "near" to the south of the Cedar River, then they were close to this McDonald's parking lot. If, however, they were "near" to the north of that confluence, then they would be paddling in what is

A reduction of the full-page P-I Lake-to-Sound story

Courtesy of Mrs Herbert Coe

Another scene, from a postcard, of the Post-Intelligencer's Black River excursion.

Canoeing on Black River, Washington.

now the middle of the main runway of the Renton Airport.

In 1912 the Cedar River was diverted into Lake Washington and four years later the Black River dried up when its source, the lake, was dropped nine feet with the opening of the Lake Washington Ship Canal. But before all that, this was the way "From Lake To Sound" and it was best done this way, in a canoe or shallow-bottomed rowboat.

And it took all day. As the text to the old photo feature explains, this group started after 11 a.m. and never made it. At 9 p.m., in the dark and exhausted, they stepped ashore at Georgetown, a few miles short of their goal, the Seattle waterfront. In 1906 the Duwamish River was not yet straightened into a waterway, and so still serpentined its way through Georgetown, which it now misses by a mile.

Although the Black River is now lost for good, there is still satisfaction in having found this inviting photograph of it.

Somewhere along the Black River.
Photo by William Boyd.

39   Flood and Famine

At 8:30 on the Sunday morning of November 19, 1911, the church bells of Renton began to peal too early for a call to worship. Indeed, earlier that morning church services had been called off, for during the night the Cedar River that normally ran through the town began to run over it.

The bells were joined by the Renton coal mine's siren whose shriek, as one old Rentonite remembered, "could run up and down five octaves and raise the hair on the back of your neck." This was the signal that 28 miles upstream the Cedar River dam had burst, releasing eleven square miles of fresh mountain water impounded behind it in the City of Seattle's reservoir.

The Monday morning *Post-Intelligencer* reported that "extraordinary sights ensued" as Renton "fled pell mell to the hills...Stampeding horses galloped along the streets, barely held in control by their struggling drivers...Sons carrying their old mothers on their shoulders...Women with bundles on their heads, dragging their children behind...

while baggage-laden fathers followed."

From the Renton Hills they looked back at their deserted town and waited for the disaster to suddenly drown it.

It was a false alarm. The dam had not burst, and there was no wall of water. By noon many of those who fled in the morning waded back to their homes to peer into flooded basements or to gather

floating woodpiles—until 3:30 that afternoon when the siren wailed again and the scene of flight was repeated.

This time the dam did break, but those who felt its main effects were in Seattle not Renton. Only the dam's top timbers gave way but the ensuing erosion undermined the bridge at Landsburg, a short way down stream from the dam, and with it the pipelines that fed Seattle its water.

Seattle media-man Daniel Patterson and adviser confer during a Renton stroll.

Thus, the Renton flood was followed by the Seattle water famine. Soon the warm Chinook winds that had brought seven inches of rain in two days and melted the early snows turned cold. The waters receded; but while Renton was shoveling mud from its basements, Seattle was filling its bathtubs with lake, spring and rain water—or any kind of water it could get.

Private water merchants sold it for 5 cents a gallon. The mayor encouraged citizens to put washtubs under their downspouts, and when the city dispatched 24 water wagons into the streets, "they were besieged by hundreds of men and women armed with receptacles of every sort."

It took a week to repair the pipes, and every dry day the warnings of the city's health commissioner were quoted on the papers' front pages, "BOIL YOUR WATER!" Seattle's schools were closed for want of steam heat, and on Wednesday 2,000 bundles of Seattle's dirty laundry were shipped to Tacoma.

The limited supply of fresh water in the city's reservoirs on Beacon and Capitol hills was directed to the business district. The *P.I.* reported, "Entire families in the dry districts have deserted their homes." Seattle's hotels were filled with visitors from Seattle. "Downtown cafes are feeding capacity crowds."

At week's end the Saturday *P.I.* reported, "Cedar River Pipe Ready To Shoot Water to City." It was the last front-page story on the event. By then Renton's flood was almost dried up, and on Sunday its citizens could, if they wanted, respond to a regular call to worship without running for the hills.

"the wake of the flood" Renton Wash. Nov. 1911.

Cedar River Between M.W. Farm & Elliott.

Copyright 1909 By W.M. Horton Lake Washington From Renton

40 Seattle's Long Branch

For a few thousand years winds and tides have been manufacturing a fine sand on West Seattle's Alki Beach. Its exposed and rather shallow shore has made an excellent resort but a lousy port.

Yet it was the port that the original settler, Charles Terry, was looking for when he stepped ashore here with the Denny Party in November 1851. Terry had visions of turning this beach into a big city and almost immediately opened the New York Cash Store on this exposed point.

When the Dennys, Borens, and Bells left it to found and settle Seattle, Charles and his brother Lee embraced it and named the whole peninsula New York after their home town. For the younger Lee it was probably homesickness that motivated the naming for he soon returned to the real Gotham. But the enterprising Charles stayed on his point New York and sold necessities like grind-

stones and brandy. It was a good place from which to spot customers.

And the customers could see the point, however, some of them didn't share Terry's big-city vision. So, to his name they added the Indian-trade-talk word for "in a while." It stuck, and for awhile it was New York-Alki or New York-in-awhile (or bye and bye) before the point became just plain Alki.

In the summer of 1852 while Terry was in his New York-Alki selling brogan shoes and hard bread to the settlers who didn't have their own stores, the real New Yorkers were escaping the heat of Manhattan for the recreational sands of a New Jersey resort named Long Branch. Ironically, 50 years later West Seattle's beach would be compared to this New Jersey resort and not New York.

In 1902 the hottest trading on Alki was not in hickory shirts but in bathing suits. Under the heading "Bathing At West Seattle Draws the Summer Crowds,"

a summer edition of the *Seattle Newsletter* drew this analogy: West Seattle is to Seattle what Long Branch is to New York—the haven of the Sunday crowds and an ideal bathing resort."

This historical beach scene accompanied that article, which went on to say, "The Seattleite sweltering from the sun's warm rays can within 15 minutes reach West Seattle and enjoy a swim along as fine a beach to be found anywhere in the world. A welcome breeze is always present from Duwamish Head to Alki Point. For three miles the beach is lined and dotted with tents, with here and there frame refreshment houses, bath houses, dime side shows, merry-go-rounds, ice cream stands and sandwich counters. It is estimated that at least 2,000 people are camping on the beach this summer and on pleasant Sundays the ferry carries hundreds who merely go to see the sights, bathe, buy red lemonade and peanuts...there is really no inconvenience in coming from and returning to town."

The *Newsletter* predicted, "Some day, when a driveway is built along the shoreline connecting the ferry landing, or with a road circling the head of the bay, Seattle's Long Branch will be an even more extensively visited resort."

The Alki Natatorium, the last of the West Seattle waterfront indoor swimming pools—abandoned. *(photo. courtesy of Don Myers.)*

Wave breaking over Seawall - Alki Bath-house - Seattle.

41   West Seattle's Harbor

Part of the industry that once moved along West Seattle's side of Elliott Bay is layered in this historical scene. From the pool room below to the Beacon Hill horizon, we cross a Northern Pacific Railroad siding, the Ferry Street Terminal (with ferry), the Seattle Yacht Club (with about 50 vessels), a flour mill (its tallest tower punctures Pigeon Point) and much more.

Even more is just out of the picture. To its left there was a drydock, boathouse, and the sprawling amusement center, Luna Park, at the tip of Duwamish Head. And from the head to the lantern at Alki Point, this recreational business district continued with a string of shacks, lean-tos, cottages, bathhouses, and concession stands that supported Seattle's summer desire to escape to the beaches of West Seattle.

1890s when it was still intact, if you missed the last ferry from Seattle at 7 p.m., you had to walk the trestle.)

Just above the last of the viaduct we can faintly see the twin stacks of a dredger and its elevated pipeline running off to the left. It is in the business of building Harbor Island. Paralleling and just above this pipeline is the larger line of the Spokane St. viaduct which ran between Pigeon Point and Beacon Hill.

But Ewing's dream of an industrial waterfront with giant wharfs providing

Left The Seattle Yacht Club when it was still at West Seattle. *Below* A detail from the primary harbor scene showing, top to bottom, Pigeon Point, the Spokane St. bridge, the Novelty Flour Mill and the West Seattle Ferry dock.

In 1907, the year West Seattle incorporated into the rest of the city, the balance of its shoreline economy leaned toward the playful. And beginning that year it was also a lot easier getting to the fun. Trolley service across the Spokane St. viaduct was completed and the double-decker *West Seattle* ferry started flashing back and forth across the bay with its ten-minute and five-cent service. Here we see it in its slip, within a year or two of its inaugural service.

As the billboard on the right reveals, in 1908-or-9, it was still possible to buy "Good View Lots" on an "Easy Payment Plan" from William Hainsworth Jr. His parent's family was one of the first on the bluff, moving there in 1889.

That was the year that West Seattle was created out of a logged-off area of second growth scrub, three-foot-thick stumps, and the ashes of a sawmill once owned by a San Francisco capitalist named Colonel Thomas Ewing. The Hainsworths bought their view lots from the colonel and he built a ferry, ferry dock, and cable car line to carry them up the ridge to his West Seattle plat.

The colonel also had industrial dreams for his waterfront and built the flour mill, convincing the Northern Pacific Railroad to build a trestle across the Duwamish tideflats to service it. The mill is the irregular mess of buildings on the photo's upper right. A long remnant of the old viaduct runs off from it and into the bay where it drops away into a random line of isolated piles. (In the

109

an intercontinental terminus for the Union Pacific Railroad (which told him in 1890 that it would be coming up the coast to West Seattle) never materialized. And naturally, the yachtsmen, sunbathers, picnickers, and pool players made the most of it.

The Seattle Yacht Club stayed at this harbor until 1917 when the Lake Washington Ship Canal gave them fresh water moorage at their present quarters on Portage Bay. By then ferry service to West Seattle had been largely superseded by the electric trolleys that sped across their viaducts and through Harbor Island: the sprawling industrial neighborhood that was dredged from the mud of Elliott Bay and not from the shoreline of West Seattle.

Alki Point Lighthouse ~ Seattle Wash'n.

42 "Ye Light Must Not Fail"

There are not many changes to discover between these "now" and "then" photographs. The point-of-view has been adjusted a few feet for a higher tide; the lighthouse has an added touch or two; the seawall has grown a few boulders; but the beach has lost its natural mess of driftwood.

The Alki Point lighthouse was constructed in 1912 and completed the following year. The historical photo dates from then. The guard fence is not yet up, and the ladder leaning against the lighthouse's west wall (on the right) leads to an oil lantern which may have been used, during construction, as a temporary warning beacon to Mosquito Fleet steamers slipping through the night between Seattle and Tacoma.

Alki's first warning light was also just a simple lantern hung from a pole. Sometime in the mid-1870s Hans Martin Hanson, who in 1868 bought the point from pioneer Doc Maynard, began his public service of lighting that lantern every night—or encouraging his son Edmund to do it.

Edmund soon passed the responsibility on to his cousin Linda Olson who each night and morning precariously negotiated the planking above an old swamp that separated the sandy tip of Alki Point from the rest of the peninsula, to ignite and dowse the light, trim the wick, and polish the brass.

In 1887 the U.S. Lighthouse Service took notice and replaced the homemade beacon with a lens-lantern mounted on a scaffold. But the tending was still kept in the Hanson-Olson family when Hans Hanson was appointed the official keeper of the light. The pay was $15 a month, and it was probably Linda Olson who kept walking the plank.

Hans Hanson died in 1900, but not before he divided his land among his children. Edmund got the tip of Alki and the tender's job. Ivar Haglund was Edmund Hanson's nephew, and remembered him as an odd sort of lighthouse keeper. Edmund was a fashionable dresser with yellow gloves, top hat, and cane and, like Ivar (who was an uncommon sort of fish-seller), he wrote jingles and told stories to the accompaniment of his guitar. Ivar remembered these performances as "incredible, but of the sheerest delight." The young nephew was, no doubt, both charmed and influenced.

In 1911 Edmund sold the point to the U.S. Lighthouse Service, and with the $9,999 he gained, took his wife, children, and guitar on an extended vacation to California. By 1913, the 37-ft. octagonal tower was up and its light flashing every second for five seconds followed by five seconds of darkness.

The Alki light was converted to electricity in 1918, and 21 years later its control and keeping were handed over to the Coast Guard. In October 1984, its operation was made fully automatic.

Its last officer in manual charge was Coast Guardsman Andrew Roberts. (Roberts stands on the bulkhead at the right of the contemporary scene.) Roberts, who must have one of the Coast Guards' better billets, now caretakes the grounds and leads weekend tours of the tower. Visitors are invited to sign in on the lighthouse log and make their comments.

There, many pages earlier, in 1954, H. Nelms wrote, "Looked on by ye landlubbers with but a passing glance, looked on by ye seafarers as a beacon of hope, ye light must not fail."

Courtesy of Michael Maslan

THE ALKI POINT LIGHTHOUSE—Within the city limits of Seattle marking the entrance to Elliott Bay   Reached by Alki street car line

Coast Guardsman Andrew Roberts and his Alki Light.

Courtesy of Frederick Mann

43   West Point Waders

On December 1, 1981 Northwest historian Murray Morgan and I took a trip for oral history. Carrying a tape recorder and a stack of photographs, we were driven to Port Townsend by architect Frederick Mann to interview his friend, and soon ours, Laura Kiehl.

Laura was born there on November 15, 1892, or 89 years and 16 days before our visit. Port Townsend, preserved as Puget Sound's 19th-Century museum, had not really changed much, nor had Laura. In her 90th year, she displayed the spontaneous wit we hope for in an intelligent young adult. Now listening to her taped commentaries pleasantly reminds me of that.

At the age of four, Laura and her younger sister, Lorena, moved to Seattle with their parents. Her father, Ambrose Kiehl, had been hired by the Army to survey the wilderness that is now Magnolia

Bluff's Discovery Park and help erect the fort which local politicians hoped would pour military money into the city's cash registers and also help defend Seattle against the rowdy radicals then milling about the city's economically distressed streets.

Ambrose, a civil engineer, who paid his way through college playing a pipe organ, did his work well. He helped design and build Fort Lawton which in the varied harmonies it strikes, with its magnificent setting, imaginatively departed from the traditional and dull rectilinear military post design.

So the engineer was also an artist. While working on the fort he served as music director of Seattle's First Baptist Church. And he was a photographer who with his several cameras built an elaborately indexed and ordered record of the growth of his family and fort. The photographs we carried to Port Townsend for Laura's commentary were printed from her father's negatives. This scene is one of them and Laura remembered it well.

Laura, second from the left, stirs the water between her mother Louisa and her sister Lorena. She explains that the other three women "in the costume of the day are guests, not relatives." The six are

Above Laura Kiehl poses with Frederick Mann and Murray Morgan during our visit with her in Port Townsend.

Below and Right early and late views of the West Point Light.

Courtesy of Lawton Gowey

Courtesy of Frederick Mann

over what a wonderful park it would make.

The Kiehls had been treating it as a park all along. For years they used this beach below the fort to entertain family and friends with clam and salmon bakes and, of course, wading.

Getting to the beach then required a long hike on a path bordered by salmon berries, devil's club, and nettles and patrolled by giant mosquitoes. Today the nettles are cleared from the path, but the beach is still protected from the summer swarms at Golden Gardens and Alki Beach by that long hike through the park. You must put out to play in these sun-warmed tidepools, for only parents with toddlers can get a pass to motor in and park beside the old lighthouse which has been warning ships away from these shallows since 1881.

Laura Kiehl graduated from the University of Washington in 1916. Later, she became the first woman in the state to be issued a brokerage license of her own. Since no brokerage house would hire her then because of her sex, she successfully operated her own office for years in the Smith Tower. She died in January 1982, less than two months after our visit.

wading in the tideflats off the southern shore of West Point. That's the still-forested Magnolia Bluff on the left and, on the right, West Seattle is just discernible through the haze across Elliott Bay.

Laura is a young teenager here. She was always tall for her age. The date is close to 1908, the last year of major construction at Fort Lawton before World War II when it briefly flourished as the second largest point of embarkation on the West Coast. By 1908 it became clear that this fort would never really be a big one, and the locals soon started musing

And the Ft. Lawton Brass Band plays on a miserably wet parade ground.

Right On the Discovery Park trail (with Alice) to the Westpoint beach (Wonderland?)

Below A contemporary picnic upon the sandy slopes above the Discovery Park bluffs with the half-moon of Ft Lawton's radar "rising" on the horizon.

Courtesy of University of Washington Historical Photography Collection

44 Looking Back at Belltown

The remarkable aspect of this photographic classic is that it was shot. Taken from the top of Denny Hill, it turns its back on the popular southern panorama to the city and Mt. Rainier for a rare look north at the rest of the hill, which in 1882 was a mess of scarred stumps and one- and two-story clapboards. Actually, the homes that run through the center of the scene are not scattered but all-in-a-row and waiting for Second Ave. to straighten itself.

That is Second on the left, twisting its way to the house on top, just right of center and a hundred or so feet beyond Lenora St. which was still another rutted by-way. That's the back hump of Denny Hill. The picture was taken from the front hump; the hill was said to resemble a camel. The valley between them, at the picture's bottom, is the future route of Virginia St.

All this figuring puts the pioneer photographer C. E. Watkins mid-block between Virginia and Stewart streets, and Second and Third avenues. It also sets him somewhere in the air more than 100 ft. higher than the alley that now runs there behind the Josephinum Catholic retirement home (once the Washington Hotel) and the rear stage door of the Moore Theater at Virginia Street.

The fact that neither hump of Denny Hill is still supporting tripods is the result of the insistent work of a city engineer named Reginald Thomson. He called this hill "an offense to the public." Thomson arrived in Seattle one year before this picture was taken and almost immediately began promoting the hill's destruction. In his autobiography he recalled "I felt that Seattle was in a pit, that to get anywhere we would be compelled to climb out of it, if we could."

And Thomson could. By 1910 everything you see here was reduced to the nondescript slopes we now call the Denny Regrade. The engineer boasted that 141 ft. had been cut away at Third Ave. "beneath the concrete floor of the Washington Hotel." That was the old castle-like Washington Hotel, built in 1891. It straddled Third Ave. between Stewart St. and Yesler Way. Since the contemporary photo was taken from the 14th floor of the "new" Washington Hotel (the Josephinum), that puts the perspective of our "now" and "then" shots very close to one another.

To Thomson's credit nothing else about them is close. He got rid of the hill because "there was much fair land for city building to the north of the hill in rather close proximity to Bell Street." Now we can see the results. Not only Belltown but Queen Anne and Magnolia are north of the hill and looking like parts of the city.

Of course, it would be absurd to suggest that north Seattle would still be wild if little Denny Hill had not been graded away. Yet now we know that the hill was a natural resource and should have been left to add character to the cityscape and pleasant views to any who scaled its modest heights or settled there.

Two who did were Major Edward Sturgis Ingraham and Dr. Orlaneo G. Root. The doctor lived in the home with the tower on the photo's far left. Root was a wonderfully appropriate name for a homeopathic physician given to prescribing herbs. He also served as the city's health officer and the county's coroner.

Major Ingraham was actually a colonel, but preferred being addressed with the lesser rank because there were so many colonels around. Ingraham was truly a splendid character. Ten days after he arrived in Seattle in 1875 as a 23-year-old classics graduate, he was made principal of the city's Central School. Later he was made superintendent of all city schools. And he was heroic. In 1888 as a member of the third party to reach

Above Turn-of-century Belltown looking south across Battery St. *Top* Looking north on 3rd Ave. across Virginia St. from the site of the Denny Hotel, ca 1890. *Bottom* Belltown north of Virginia St. during the 1916 snow.

the summit of Mt. Rainier, he spent a night in the steam caves. Ingraham obviously liked heights, even modest ones like from "Mt. Denny." His home is the two-story box on the horizon left of the picture's center.

45 Seattle, 1885

This historical view was photographed 99 years ago from the southern slope of Denny Hill. It was then that Arthur Denny began referring to this high point on his original claim as Capitol Hill. He hoped to kidnap the territorial capitol from Olympia and build its new home here.

The rear of Arthur Denny's own home at First Ave. and Union St. is the string of white additions beneath the puff of white smoke on the panorama's far right. Union St. cuts across the center of this scene, and the paralleling Pike St. is below it. Second Ave. rises out of the photograph's bottom right-hand corner, and Third Ave. symmetrically ascends from the lower left.

This was residential Seattle, circa 1885. The commercial district around

Courtesy of University of Washington Historical Photography Collection

Pioneer Square is to the photograph's distant upper-right. Beyond that the tide is in and laps against the western side of Beacon Hill, the long ridge on the horizon.

In this neighborhood the humbler homes were mixed in with a few mansions, and most of the lots were large ones. There was room enough for a generous garden, a few fruit trees, and a lawn. In Denny's case, a backyard pasture was reserved for the family's milk cow. Private lots were usually separated from each other and the city's elevated wood plank sidewalks by picket fences, in some shade of white. In 1885 the dirt streets were narrower yet only recently regraded from their original condition of bumpy stump-strewn paths. Second Ave. was smoothed out in 1883, and in 1884 tracks for the city's first horse-drawn streetcar were laid up its center. They can

be seen on the right in the block between Union and Pike.

Of the seven churches in this panorama, the only obvious one is the Swedish Lutheran Evangelical Gethsemane Congregation on the lower left at Third Ave. and Pike St. Dedicated on February 22, 1885 it was Seattle's first

TERRITORIAL UNIVERSITY.

Scandinavian and Lutheran church and its pastor, Dr. G. A. Anderson, spent alternate Sundays here and in Tacoma.

Above the church is Denny's Knoll, the site since 1861 of the Territorial University, the large white structure topped with a cupola and fronted by Doric columns. To the rear and left of the

121

university is Providence Hospital (at the present site of the Federal Courthouse.)

Below and to the photographer's side of the school and half hidden behind firs is the three-story white home of the Young Naturalists Club. This fraternity of scientifically curious specimen collectors was the beginning of the Washington State Museum. In 1985, it celebrated its centennial in its present home on the U.W. campus, the Burke Museum.

For all the familiar charm that seems to pervade this mid-1880s scene, the year 1885 was remembered by Thomas Prosch, then the *Post Intelligencer*'s editor, as characterized by "a great deal of ugly feeling...the times were hard and the hands of all seemed to be raised against others. Grievances were common and relief measures took violent shape."

The economic depression that followed the crash of 1883 kept the times dull. Although the new transcontinental railroad brought west a hopeful flood of single men looking for work, what they found were opportunities that required not labor but cash. The result was a volatile split between labor and capital that erupted into race riots in Tacoma and Seattle. The scapegoats of

Courtesy of Lawton Gowey

Above Only thirty odd years separates this view towards the razed Denny Knoll from that printed in the left panel on the preceeding pages. Here the corner of Third & Pine is on the lower left.

the working mens' resentment were the Chinese and the capitalists who exploited their relatively cheap labor.

The 1984 view was photographed neither from the state capitol, as Arthur Denny would have liked it, nor from his namesake hill. This part of it was flattened in 1906.

This panorama from Denny Hill was photographed *ca* 1884 or about one year earlier than that printed on the preceeding pages. The bonfire, right of center, is burning on Second Ave. midway between Union and Pike Streets. The pier jutting into Elliott Bay, upper right, is the King St. coal wharf. Below it is Yesler's Wharf.

46 When Third Avenue Was Church Row

In 1890, Seattle was rebuilding from the Great Fire of the year before that had destroyed most of the young city's business district. Thousands of immigrants and entrepreneurs using millions in eastern and local capital constructed hundreds of new buildings every year until the international crash of 1893 forestalled the boom.

It was the recently completed transcontinental Northern Pacific Railroad that brought most of the opportunists west. The railroad's own official photographer, Jay Haynes, also came to town in 1890 to record the phenomenal growth.

Both of our historical images were taken by Haynes during that visit. In the

main photograph, his view is to the south on Third Ave., across the Madison St. intersection. In the other image, Haynes went one block south on Third Ave. and shot across the street to the Stacy mansion at the northeast corner of Marion St.

Seattle in 1890 was booming, but not Third Ave. This was Church Row where the spirit held steady just beyond the pale of the commercial rush down on Second and First avenues and south of Yesler Way.

Earlier, in the 1880s, another spirit moved a few of the congregations over from Second Ave. As businesses invaded east from First Ave., the elders sold their church properties for a profit, sufficient to relocate to grander sanctuaries on the more meditative Third Ave.

So it was for the Methodist

Courtesy of University of Washington Historical Photography Collection

Courtesy of Seattle Public Library

Above The Stacy Mansion when it still faced 3rd Ave at Marion St., 1890.

Episcopal Church, the ornate Gothic structure in the center of Haynes' view. This was the second home for the Seattle congregation. Its first church was built in 1855 down on Second Ave. by its first pastor, David Blaine. When Blaine arrived in Seattle in 1853, he was also the town's principal entrepreneur with $350, or the advanced half of his first year's salary. He loaned $200 to Henry Yesler for a new mill, and assumed many of the debts involved in building the town's first house of worship, the "White

Church" at Second Ave. and Columbia St.

When the congregation moved to its new home at Third Ave. and Marion St. in 1887, the old White Church was sold and moved by its new owner also up to Third Ave., two blocks south at Cherry St. Clarence Bagley, who years earlier was married in the town's first church, noted in his *History of King County* that "it became a saloon and gambling house and the resort of lewd men and women."

The First Presbyterian Church on the left of Haynes' view did not move up

from Second Ave. It was built here at Third Ave. and Madison St. in 1876 as the first Presbyterian church in Seattle. Its pastor, George Whitworth, had come to town a decade earlier as president of the Territorial University.

In 1890 the First Presbyterian Church drew the biggest crowds in town. To accommodate the growing congregation it moved in 1893 to Fourth Ave. and Spring St. into a barn-sized sanctuary seating 1,500. By 1907 it moved to its third home at Seventh Ave. and

Spring St. where its new pastor, Mark Matthews, packed them in with a mix of hell fire and political haranguing against the vices of the city. Many a nonprofessing pagan attended Matthews' services merely for the show.

However, the speed with which the Presbyterians moved from church to church did not compare with the rate at which Martin Van Buren and Elizabeth Stacy changed residences. In 1885 they spent $50,000 they had made in lumber and real estate on the mansion that fills the block between the Methodists and Presbyterians. Its lavishly decorated Second Empire architecture with mansard roof and fourth-floor cupolas was a monument to the Stacys and competed in a secular but favorable way with the churches to the north and south. And the Stacys chose to treat it as a monument. They refused to move in until 1887, and then only for as long as it took them to build yet another home at the northeast corner of Madison and Boren.

Their move was part of a trend of the wealthy who were relocating from the central city to hilltop mansions that looked down imperially on the businesses below. Within a year the Stacys moved again to yet another home on Boren St., or at least Elizabeth moved. Through the 1890s, Mr. Stacy was listed in the city directory as residing at a variety of hotels or clubs while Elizabeth stayed up on the hill.

In 1890 the Seattle Chamber of Commerce moved into the Stacy mansion on Third Ave. and eventually the Men's University Club occupied their residence at Madison and Boren. When Martin died in 1901 and Elizabeth in 1904, they left no children and little fortune.

The 1907 regrading of Third Ave. brought the demise of Church Row. By the end of the decade the old, tree-lined street was transformed into another avenue of commerce. Both the Methodist and the Presbyterian churches were gone; only the Stacy mansion remained. In 1893 it was converted into a stylish boarding house.

Its last conversion came in the 1920s when Charles Joseph Ernest Blanc moved in, turning its imposing four stories 90 degrees to face Marion St. and opened the Maison Blanc Restaurant. For many years it served local tastes until fire hit on April 30, 1960. Two months later the last symbol of Third Ave.'s elegance was leveled.

Top The east bay-window of the Maison Blanc and, *below*, the mop-up after the 1960 fire that closed it and ultimately spelled the doom of the old landmark Stacy Mansion.

Courtesy of Lawton Gowey

St Looking North · · No 108 · LAROCHE Photo

Courtesy of Michael Maslan

47 Third and Union, 1891

This historical scene was drawn from a promotional album assembled in 1891 for Luther Griffith, then one of Seattle's most prominent capitalists, although now rarely remembered. All the album photos were shot by the pioner Seattle photographer Frank La Roche, a name we will never forget because he wrote it on all his negatives.

We don't really know if the photographer exposed this image especially for the capitalist, or whether the latter only chose it from La Roche's current stock-in-trade. Whichever, it and all the other photos in that album are up-to-date and picked to show off the progressive side of Seattle in 1891.

Griffith was trying to sell street railways; La Roche, in this photo, was showing off Seattle's then new and as yet unopened hotel on the hill. No doubt the promoter Griffith liked this urbane symbol, so here from his album we see looming above the city in the distant haze the elegant bulk of Denny Hotel atop Denny Hill.

La Roche set his tripod on the dirt of Third Ave. 70 or so yards south of Union St. He was safe. Compared to the modern rat race of internal combustion and tunnel construction that is now Third, in 1891 it was a pleasantly relaxed but dusty grade where more than one horse and buggy (on the right) could casually park the wrong way on this two-way street.

The second tower in this scene (left of center) sits atop the brick Burke Block at the northwest corner of Third and Union. On the main floor the plumber and steamfitter, A. F. Schlump, did his business. Across Union is the mansion-sized home of Charles Denny, the last vestige of the old single-family residential neighborhood.

Then, in 1891, this 1300 block of Third Ave. between University and Union streets was packed with diverse commerce. Included were a dressmaker, a hairdresser, three rooming houses, a music teacher, a mustard manufacturer, a retail druggist, a wholesale confectioner, two tobacconists, a second-hand store, a restaurant, a sewing machine store, a church (the massive Plymouth Congregational, behind the photographer at University St.), and a Mrs. Cox, who listed herself in the 1891 *Polk Business Directory* simply as "Artist."

Also at the Union St. end of this block in the Plummer Building, the two-story clapboard with the three gables on the photo's right, there was another tobaconnist, a home furnishings store, a lodging house, a saloon and the Seattle Undertakers.

Ten years later this "progress" on Third Ave. got most dramatic when the Plummer Building was picked up and moved two blocks north to Pine St. to make way for the Federal Post Office (and the P.O., although a different one, is still on the Union St. site—on the "now" photo's right.)

Beginning in 1906, Third Ave.'s forward look started looking through Denny Hill, which in the next four years would be leveled, allowing the street to pass through the Denny Regrade with barely a rise. Of course, the grand hotel, La Roche's subject and Griffith's symbol, was razed with the hill.

Courtesy of University of Washington Historical Photography Collection

Courtesy of Michael Maslan

Top When the federal government chose the 3rd & Union site for its new post office in 1901, the Plummer Bldg., top and above right, was moved up Third Ave. two blocks to the sw corner of Third and Pine.

127

Courtesy of Lawton Gowey

48   A City of Landmarks

This view from Denny Hill is 80+ years old. And although only a few residents can remember first-hand any of the landmarks in this panorama, this scene may inspire nostalgia for a neighborhood most of us have never lived in. From here the city seems like a place where one would expect to regularly cross paths with family and friends. However, we do not need to be personally homesick to longingly scan this photograph and enjoy the wonderful mix of human and natural touches.

Many of these landmarks should be familiar to readers of Seattle's photographic past. For instance, the top-heavy King County Courthouse, which pierces the upper left-hand corner of this early century skyline. This "Cruel Castle" was built in 1889 atop "Profanity Hill." For a quarter century it made judges, lawyers, and litigants alike climb the steep Terrace St. steps to reach its courtrooms on Seventh Ave.

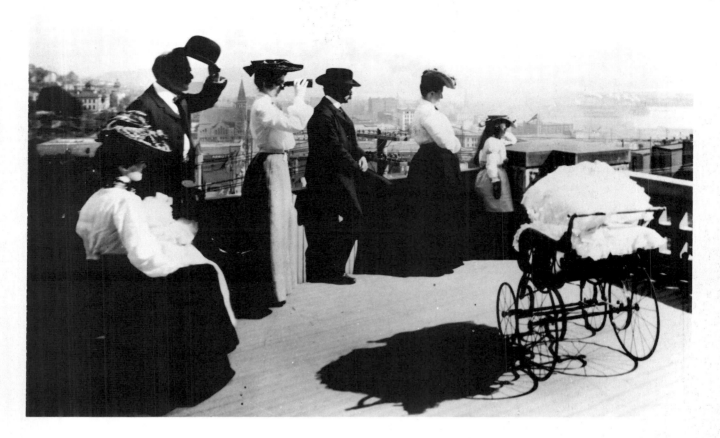

Many complained and some swore at this sweaty inconvenience. But the prisoners jailed in the west wing of the "Gray Pile" would have been quietly thankful for just one downhill opportunity at this extra-legal exercise. Unlike the judges who moved out in 1915 to the present County Courthouse at Fourth Ave. and Jefferson St., the inmates did not leave until 1931 when this "tower of despair" was brought down by dynamite.

Just below and a little to the right of the courthouse are the towers of Providence Hospital. They face Fifth Ave. between Madison and Spring streets, at the present location of the Federal Courthouse. Beneath the hospital is Denny's Knoll, the greenbelt that crosses a good portion of our panorama. When the Territorial University was first constructed here in 1861, this knoll was a clearcut patch surrounded by virgin forest. But here, only 40 years later, the scene is reversed. Now this tree-filled pastoral setting is surrounded by a city.

The knoll interrupts Fourth Ave. The university building, which at this time was the temporary headquarters for the local library, sits elegantly at what is today the northeast corner of Fourth Ave. and Seneca St., part of the present location of the Four Seasons Olympic Hotel.

The tower of the James McNaught mansion is evident just to the right of the university building. That is the present location of the Seattle Public Library.

Just below the university is the roof and portico of the Armory at the southwest corner of Fourth Ave. and Union St. Erected in 1888, and intended for National Guard drills, it was more frequently used for political conventions, bicycle races, operatic productions, wrestling matches, and, after the fire of 1889, it served briefly as city hall.

The barnlike structure just right of center is the massive First Presbyterian Church built in 1893 with 1,500 seats to accommodate the religious revivals of the 1890s. It fills the northwest corner of Fourth Ave. and Spring St. Just beyond the church and to its right, the west wall of Seattle's first apartment-hotel sticks out. The Lincoln Hotel was built in 1899 at Fourth Ave. and Madison St., the present site of the SeaFirst Tower, but stood only until

1920 when the west wall caved in to one of the city's more spectacular fires.

The high steeple to the right of the Lincoln belongs to Plymouth Congregational Church. Built in 1891, it survived the 1907 regrading of Third Ave., but not the more secular alterations of theater magnate, Alexander Pantages. In 1911 he bought the church, razed it, and put in its place his temple-like theater, the Pantages.

The slender Gothic spire to the right of the Plymouth tower is part of the Methodist Episcopal Church at Third Ave. and Marion St. The clapboard structure that dominates the foreground of our panorama is the northern anchor for this street of sanctuaries. This Methodist Protestant church was built in 1890 at the southeast corner of Third Ave. and Pine St. With the 1907 regrading of

Third Ave., the congregation moved out and the church was converted into the temporary and last home of the Third Avenue Theater. Its original home at Third Ave. and Madison St. had been leveled by the same regrading.

The last landmark noted here is the small conical tower at the bottom of the photograph. This is not attached to a nave but to a fire station. Thus, the tower is not for pointing to heaven, but for drying hoses.

The contemporary view down Third Ave. was photographed from the top floor of the public parking garage between Stewart and Virginia streets. The photographer of the historical view also straddled Third Ave., but his position was some five or six stories higher and considerably closer to Stewart St.

The panorama was taken from either the tower or the balcony above the carriage porch of the Washington Hotel. The year was most likely 1903, about the time the hotel's proprietor, James Moore, first opened it to Theodore Roosevelt's personal patronage. The hotel is evident in the second historical image, photographed from the corner of Third Ave. and Pine St.

Top This etching of Mt. Rainier looming above 3rd Ave. was drawn in early 1890 while the then towerless Methodist Episcopal Church was still under construction. *Above* Where Denny Hill began—the look up 3rd Ave. from Pike St.

SEATTLE from the HOTEL DENNY.

Third Ave. and the greenbelt along the grounds of the Territorial University in the early 1880s.

Also showing is the trolley that, in part, solved the problem of how to get guests to the "most scenic hotel in America." Moore came up with one of the better-remembered lines from local history, when he said of his block-long trolley that, "It may be the shortest in the world, but it is as wide as any."

Right James Moore's one-block-long trolley to his Denny-hotel-converted Washington Hotel. *Below* The same scene two or three years later during the 1907 leveling of both the hotel and this part of Denny Hill.

49   The Third Avenue Regrade

In a June 24, 1906 feature story, the *Post-Intelligencer* asked, "Is not Seattle regrade-mad?" Headlined, "REGRADERS ARE LEVELING SEATTLE," the story went on to explain this regrading madness to an imagined and perplexed visitor.

"The early pioneer was content to trudge up and down steep grades all day, unquestioningly, as though such things were destined to be permanent. . . . Now any hill with a valley below it suggests a regrade."

This historical scene looks up the Third Ave. regrade. The photograph was shot on a sunny winter day in 1907. The *Post-Intelligencer* story went on to explain that "Two of the most important regrades ever undertaken in Seattle are those on Third and Fourth avenues. They are the outgrowth of the wonderful expansion of Seattle's retail business.

Courtesy of Old Seattle Paperworks, Pike Place Market

With First and Second avenues congested, the retail trade must spread. . . . The depth of the cut on Third runs all the way from nothing at Cherry Street to 17 feet at Madison."

In our scene the deepest cut at Madison is below the Madison St. cable car that passes over Third Ave. on a temporary wooden trestle on the picture's far left. The pedestrian trestle in the foreground follows the line of Marion St. and reaches to the south side of the Stacy mansion on the right. No doubt, a few of you readers have had dinner in this elegant home. Its last resident was the Maison Blanc restaurant which survived until destroyed by fire in 1960.

The Third Avenue Theater at Madison St. did not survive even the Third Ave. regrade. We can see it here just to the right of the cable car, at the northeast corner of Third and Madison, the present site of the SeaFirst Tower. The home of Seattle's first stock theatrical company, it ran its fare of farce and melodrama here for 16 years until the regraded 17-foot cliff at its front door made it impossible for theater-goers to get into the show.

Up Third at University St. the digging didn't go so deep, and Plymouth Congregational Church kept its services going beneath the tall brick tower we can see rising above the cable car.

Beyond the church is the ruined half-shell of the old Denny-Washington Hotel atop Denny Hill. Within the year, 1907, "regrade-mad" Seattle would level both the front of the hill and the rest of the hotel to the grade of Third Ave.

Third Ave. is now being regraded again, with Metro's bus tunnel. The cuts will be as deep as 50 feet.

Top Third n. of Madison during the 1907 regrade with the last of the Washington Hotel in the hazy horizon. *Above* Shoveling on 3rd just south of Plymouth Congregational Church at University St. *Right* The 3rd Ave. regrade from the roof of the Alaska bldg at 2nd & Cherry.

Courtesy of Lawton Gowey

133

Below The 3rd Ave. regrade looking south from Spring St. Compare this scene to that in story
46 Church Row.

Courtesy of Lawton Gowey

Gethsemane Lutheran Church at 9th
and Stewart St.,*above. Top* Seattle
High School (Broadway Hi). *Right*
Looking back up Denny Hill from
Fifth and Olive towards Denny Hotel
from where the panorama was shot.
St. Marks Episcopal Church's first,
and here abandoned, home is in the
foreground.

Courtesy of University of Washington Historical Photography Collection

50   The View from Denny Hill to Capitol Hill

I n 1901 when Denny Hill was still in its place, there was an unobstructed view in all directions from the towers of the grand hotel on top of it. The most popular prospects were towards Mt. Rainier in the south, over the heart of what was then the fastest growing city in the American Northwest, and to the west over Elliott Bay.

Here, in this "then" is the rarer view east towards Capitol Hill. Under construction on the right horizon is the roofless Broadway High. When it was

Right 1920s view up Stewart and Olive Streets over the roof of the Times Square Bldg.

Courtesy of Lawton Gowey

The three larger views included here cover a span of only 17 or 18 years. The scene below was photographed in 1890 or 91 when there was still very little settlement on the sides of Capitol Hill. The view above as shot some little time after the scene featured on the preceeding page. Here Broadway High is completed and open and the Seattle Electric trolley barns at 6th & Olive (lower right) have expanded considerably.

The scene, lower-right, was photograhed from the roof of the New Washington Hotel (now the Josephinum) at 2nd an Stewart and dates from either 1907 or 1908. The re-grade of Denny Hill's front hump between Pine and Virginia Streets has been completed, St. Marks and the First Swedish Baptist Church have been razed, and Westlake Ave. cut through.

Courtesy of Old Seattle Paperworks, Pike Place Market

opened in the fall of 1902, it was the city's first school devoted exclusively to grades 9-through-12.

This scene is littered with landmarks, although none of them really dominates the field—except those duplexes in the lower left-hand corner. They reveal the rental character of much of old Denny Hill's neighborhood, and were razed with the hill five years after this photograph was taken.

The two streets that form a "V" through the scene are Stewart St. on the left and Olive St. in the center. (A portion of Pine St. is showing on the far right.) Fourth Ave. is at the photograph's base and the triangular block in the center foreground (bordered by Fourth, Fifth, Stewart, and Olive) is now the site of what some consider Seattle's most beautiful building: the former home of the *Seattle Times*, the Times Square Building.

In the historical view, that flatiron block is filled with the remains of St. Mark's Episcopal Church's first home. The congregation bought this fractional block in 1889 for $6,000, but moved out six years later to a bigger church on First Hill. The Gothic spire across Fifth Ave. from St. Mark's rises from the austere sanctuary of the First Swedish Baptist Church.

Indeed, this panorama is strewn with churches—about a dozen of them—although they are not easy to find. Except, that is, for Gethsemane Swedish Lutheran, the dazzling white structure, left-center. The year 1901 was its first

year at this location, Ninth and Stewart, although it was the oldest Lutheran congregation in Seattle. In 1985 they celebrated their centennial. Their first church was built in 1885 at Third Ave. near Pine.

The Stewart St. block just this side of Gethsemane in the photo is so steep that wagons had to switch back to the top. Today this block, which is sided by the Greyhound depot, is nearly level. This radical regrading followed when over 20 ft. of fill from Denny Hill was dumped onto Eighth Ave., and more than ten feet was cut away at Ninth Ave. This

last was done at a considerable expense to the Lutherans who had to lower their church.

The cut into Stewart at Fourth Ave. (in the foreground) was considerably deeper—almost 50 ft. Thus, although the contemporary photo seems to have been shot from a higher altitude, the 8th floor of the Securities Building, than the historical photographer's perch in the Denny Hotel, it wasn't.

The old hotel is almost a subject of the older scene. On the lower-left, the afternoon sun casts its tower's shadow across Fourth Ave.

Courtesy of Lawton Gowey

Courtesy of University of Washington Historical Photography Collection

51   Double Take from Denny Hill

About 1884 or 5 local photographer Theodore Pieser lugged his equipment up the stumpy southern side of Denny Hill. There he might have turned around to photograph one of the many mid-1880s panoramic views of the city which still survive. Thankfully, Pieser did the unexpected and shot north to the "suburbs."

Five or six years later, in 1890, the traveling photographer F. Jay Haynes steadied his tripod at near the same location and also shot north. The difference between what Pieser and Haynes saw is a startling indication of what can happen to a booming western town in only a few adolescent years. (For more views north from this location, turn the page.)

In Pieser's view, the tall firs in the center of the photograph are arranged like a scruffy windbreaker against the

wind off Lake Union. They line the ridge that runs north and south between today's Boren and Terry avenues. The trees screen the northern end of Capitol Hill but in the Haynes' scene, they have been cleared away probably as timber for David Denny's Western Mill at the south end of Lake Union, evident center-left in both historical photos.

Both panoramas look north from Fifth or Sixth Avenues and Virginia St. In Pieser's view the irregular development along rough paths has in Haynes' scene been platted. It assumes an urban shape. The most prominent street descendng from the ridge, center-right, is Lenora. It drops down from Boren Ave. to where Westlake will 15 years later be cut through from Fourth Ave. and Pike St. It will follow near the line of the old mid-1870s narrow-gauge coal road that ran in the Westlake ravine from Lake Union to the Pike St. coal wharf.

The boxish home in the center of Pieser's photograph is also seen in Haynes' view. Lenora St. seems to run into its roof. In 1890 Lenora ran out of Denny Way, again, at the top of the ridge. Denny Way continues on west, cutting into the ridge as it descends to Westlake, which has from that point been graded through to the lake.

In both views we can scan the long sheds of the Western Mill Co. and the small surrounding community. Here, only a few years earlier, David and Louisa Denny pastured their cows and hunted

wild duck. The mill was opened in 1882, about the time a boardwalk, 3-feet-wide and 4,531-feet-long was built from Pike St. to Lake Union.

In 1885 Denny became the mill's principal stockholder. But after the international market crash of 1893, David Denny lost it to John Brace, one of his

employees. (There is still a Brace Lumber Co. at the foot of Westlake Ave.)

In 1885, 223 bodies were removed from the city cemetery, which was then renamed Denny Park. It is still one block west of Westlake Ave., or just to the left of both our panoramas. A year earlier, in 1884, the city made a brave decision to

Courtesy of University of Washington Historical Photography Collection

build a school in its northern suburbs—a block west of the Denny cemetery-park, at the location of the *Post-Intelligencer* until its recent move to the waterfront. It too was called Denny, and although not present in Pieser's photograph, its prominent bell tower was surely visible to him from this perch.

Three-thousand, two hundred and eighteen votes were cast in the November election of 1884; one quarter of them by the newly, but briefly, enfranchised women. They saw to it that the majority of offices were filled by "sober, honest, and efficient men who favor the enforcement of existing laws and ordinances." Progressive Seattle was now the territory's largest town, but its future in all directions, north included, was uncertain. For in 1884 the "Seattle Spirit" was having an anxiety attack caused primarily by the "City of Destiny" to the south, Tacoma. There the November vote total was only 1,663, but they were all for the Northern Pacific Railroad.

Tacoma was a company town, and the company did not care for Seattle. Nearly every intervening moment between Pieser's and Haynes' visit to the same north Seattle spot was filled locally with preoccupations on how to keep the town growing in spite of the active hostility of the Northern Pacific Railroad. Seattle was separated from regular connection with the railroad's transcontinental service which terminated at Tacoma.

How this struggle progressed is partly revealed in the dynamic differences between Pieser's and Haynes' panoramas. It was also witnessed by Haynes himself, who was sent to Seattle and the eastern slope of Denny Hill by his employer, the Northern Pacific Railroad.

In 1890 this wide view north across William Bell's and David Denny's claims was also a Northern Pacific view, for early that year the railroad began full and equal service to the "Queen City of Puget Sound," equal to that given "The City of Destiny," Tacoma.

Right Three more views from Denny Hill with their estimated dates, top to bottom, 1887, 1888, 1891. *Upper-left* is the interior of Northern Pacific photographer Jay Haynes private coach, and *bottom left* an 1884 birds-eye view to the general location for all five panoramas. (Arrow marks the spot.)

142

52   David Denny's Empire

Casually hooking a thumb in his pants pocket, pioneer David Denny poses on car #1 of his Rainier Power & Railway Company's new electric trolley line. The car, no doubt, has also paused to pose for the photographer, although the motorman to Denny's right has one hand on the throttle and the other on the brake preparing for opportunities or emergencies up the line.

At the car's far end is David Denny Jr., an electrical engineer and so enthusiastic partner with his father in this state-of-the-electrical-art conveyance. The scene is at the southeast corner of Lake Union and the year either 1892 or 3—four decades since the older Denny came here as a teenager in the fall of 1851 and almost immediately started building the first settler's cabin on Elliott Bay at Alki point. Here he is turning 60 and looking, at last, to build his empire in North Seattle.

Of course, EMPIRE was the boom call of the times in the American West and so certainly in Seattle, the fastest growing city in the Northwest, and so reasonably also in North Seattle and David Denny's part of it at the south end of Lake Union.

When the city started to spread his way, David Denny gave empire-sounding names to his enterprises, starting with the Western Mill which, when it was built in the early 1880s, was the largest in King County. Denny named his real estate business, the Washington Improvement Company; his waterworks, the Union Water Company; and his electrical railway he grandiloquently, but safely, named after the mountain. So in the early 1890s David Denny was ready and willing for empire.

And so was the "Empire Builder," James J. Hill. Hill had promised Seattle that once his transcontinental Great Northern was completed to this city in 1893, he would come west accompanied by "three hundred men who would represent a thousand millions of money, and reveal to them a virgin field of enterprise...whose resources and reasonable expectations exceed those of any other section of the country."

David Denny's "reasonable expectations" were for Latona and Brooklyn, the names of neighborhoods on his trolley line, now known as Wallingford and the University District. He wanted the eastern capitalists to ride his railroad and seed his "virgin field."

Instead, as the photograph shows and perhaps heralds, his electric cars were usually empty, and the Denny family's dream of empire collapsed into the nightmare of bankruptcy. As Gordon Newell records in his biography of David Denny, *Westward to Alki*, "It was the long-remembered Panic of 1893 that wiped out the fruits of more than four decades of privation, danger and toil... Everything he owned was soon swept

144

into the financial whirlpool that rose around him."

Of course, many other booms went bust. Land depreciated as much as 80%, and about the only property transferred was to the sheriff for debts or to the state treasurer for taxes. Almost all the city's street railways went into receivership, as did all but one of the eight railroads operating in and about Seattle. The exception was the "empire builder's" Great Northern, which was then not carrying much empire anywhere and yet was surviving.

Of the 23 banks in King County, only 9 survived. One of these was Seattle's oldest, Dexter Horton's, for which David Denny's older brother, Arthur, was the senior vice president.

Probably the saddest sign of how the Seattle of the 1850s, a village of a few families and helping friends, had transformed into an exploding metropolis of competing strangers was that David Denny's brother's bank was one of the creditors standing in line to force his bankruptcy.

Courtesy of Lawton Gowey

Westlake Ave. proceeds north from Denny Way just above the center of this scene. There it passes through David Denny's "empire" and to his Western Mill on the southern shore of Lake Union.

53 Decatur Terrace

When, at last David and Louisa Denny built themselves a proper mansion they set it on a terrace high above the intersection of Mercer St. and Temperance Ave. (their prohibitionist name for what is now Queen Anne Ave.). Their wide front porch looked west across their claim towards Elliott Bay and the spot, near the foot of Denny Way, where only 40 years before the pioneering couple had built a log cabin in the forest wilderness.

They named their mansion "Decatur Terrace" after a fort which was their (and the rest of Seattle's) protection during the Indian War of 1856. The locals named their blockhouse at the foot of Cherry St. after the *U.S.S. Decatur* which was, happily for them, well-armed and then just off shore on Elliott Bay.

On the morning of January 26, 1856, the sloop *Decatur* sent a howitzer shot screaming across the rooftops of Seattle and into the forest—at what is now Third Ave. The natives hiding there answered with hollers and a barrage of small arms fire. The villagers responded by dashing into their fort. And there they sat out the Battle of Seattle. Actually, it was over by nightfall, but the residents couldn't be sure of that, so they held up in the blockhouse for a few weeks more—long enough for Louisa Denny to give birth in March to her second daughter Madge.

The baby was baptized Madge Decatur Denny, so the mansion was also named after their daughter. Madge died in 1888 after a brief illness. She never saw her namesake mansion which was built in the early 1890s, nor could she attend the magnificent home's one grand night on January 23, 1895—the 42nd wedding anniversary of the first couple married in King County. The celebrants included the surviving five of Denny's eight children, nine grandchildren, and most of what was left of pioneer Seattle: the Bagleys, Mercers, Blaines, and Kelloggs.

The wedding invitations were inscribed on fringed buckskin, and the mansion was decorated with pioneer articles like powder horns, calico sunbonnets, and a rough table set with a smoked salmon, a tin plate of boiled potatoes, a few sea biscuits and clams.

The *Post-Intelligencer's* detailed report noted that "The chief diversion was afforded by the sudden entrance of a band of 16 young men and women gorgeously dressed as Indians...They sat in a circle with their 'tamanuse' boards upon which they played the old-time music and sang their Indian songs."

David Denny reflected for the pioneer group how "People in these days of modern improvements and plenty know nothing of the hardships the pioneer of 40 years ago had to undergo right here...It was a life of privations, inconveniences, anxieties, fears, and dangers innumerable, and required physical and mental strength to live it out."

One of the Denny grandchildren recited a special poem which ended optimistically "In good new times not far away/ May people smiling and people say,/ 'Heaven bless their coming years'/ Honor the noble pioneers.'"

But not all was as it seemed. This anniversary was shrouded in an irony so powerful that the *P.I.* story could not mention it for fear of breaking the charm. Most of those attending surely felt it and also tried to suppress the foreboding that within the year David and Louisa Denny would be kicked out of their mansion. Decatur Terrace was ultimately no fort against the two-year barrage of bankruptcy that followed the market crash of 1893.

This splendid Gothic pile was the last of David Denny's many civilizing successes to go. When he left he paused at the door, looked about and remarked, "I'll never look upon Seattle again..."

David and Louisa then moved in with their daughter Emily at Licton Springs. From there he returned to the wilderness of the Cascades to prospect for gold.

David Denny died November 25, 1903. Louisa lived on 13 years more. Their repossessed mansion was later moved one block south to Republican St. (another of David Denny's street names) and converted into apartments.

Courtesy of Seattle Engineering Dept.

Looking east form Boren and John to the last of Denny Hill. This four-part panorama extends from Queen Anne Hill on the right to the Central Business District on the left. The dominant topographical oddity pictured here is the cliff along the west side of 9th Ave. and the treeline of Denny Park above it, at its old pre-regrade elevation.

54   The Old Quarter

On the unseasonably hot Monday morning of May 7, 1928 a photographer from the city's engineering department shot the last days of old Denny Hill, or what was then still left of it. By 1911 Denny Hill's highest half (that west of Fifth Ave.) was regraded to its modern level, and the old hill neighborhood that survived (east of Fifth) was considered ultimately doomed. But although its days were numbered, they stretched on for years.

The result was that for nearly two decades it was left untouched, unofficially sealed off from progress and "improvements," waiting for demolition and in the meantime growing beautifully weathered. It was described as "floating like a somnolent island in the roaring sea of downtown."

The city's photographer aimed to the west across Westlake (below) from near John and Boren streets. Turning to make four consecutive shots he recorded a complete panorama of what the regraders called "a hideous monument to work only partly finished." The one-fourth we feature here shows the hill's real monuments on its horizon. The tower right-of-center sits atop Denny School at Sixth and Battery. Left-of-center is the brick spire of Sacred Heart Parish at Sixth and Bell.

The school was built in 1883-4, so in 1928 it was the oldest in Seattle. And the parish, established here in 1889, was formerly part of the city's first Catholic church, Our Lady Of Good Help. When the latter disbanded, Sacred Heart became, by its birthright, the city's oldest Catholic parish.

But with the regrades, rumors of regrades, and the northerly expansion of used car dealerships, the old neighborhood of worshippers and students that once filled the church's pews and sat upon the school's stools was reduced to

Courtesy of Seattle Engineering Dept.

this enclave. The part we see here lay south and alongside Denny Park which is on the photo's right. The cliff along Ninth Ave. (also on the right) still prevented Denny Way from cutting a paved swath between them.

On December 1, 1925 the city council agreed to go ahead with leveling the rest of Denny Hill. But for three years more the district's 150 property owners and their three dozen lawyers kept the condemnation settlements in the courts. Meanwhile the time-capsule neighborhood continued to weather.

In February 1927 a *Seattle Times* reporter visited Seattle's "old quarter" and discovered a "paradise for children, where boys play marbles in the middle of Sixth Avenue." The writer noted that the locals refer to their quarter of "unpaved streets, unpainted houses and absence of traffic" as their "free city." Describing Denny Park, the reporter wrote "Here on Sundays come working folk from the houses off Westlake Ave. below to read their newspapers, eat their lunches and doze the afternoon away...It is one of our last downtown breathing places." And it still is, although now some 40 ft. lower.

Courtesy of University of Washington Historical Photography Collection

Above A late 1880s view of Denny School at Fifth and Battery. *Right* after the 1929 regrade the Denny school's bell tower was set in Denny Park. *Below* The "First shovel to use the 5th Ave. Conveyor Belt."

At last on February 20, 1929 a steam shovel took its first bite into the remains of Denny Hill. It did it in the name of progress and just in time for the Great Depression that humbled practically everything and everybody later that year.

When post-World War II progress reached the regrade, it laid out a charmless expanse of parking lots and mostly cheap constructions, a few of which rank among the city's ugliest.

1st Shovel At Conveyor
5th Ave. + Battery St.

7483
5-11-29

Courtesy of Seattle Engineering Dept.

Above The old Denny Park at its pre-regrade level. *Below* The "Old Quarter" and Denny Park, seperated from a more commercial neighborhood by Westlake Ave.

Courtesy of Seattle Engineering Dept.

55 The Last of Denny Hill

The popular impression that Denny Hill was reconstituted as Harbor Island in the tideflats south of town is myth. Most of Denny Hill wound up where the dirt piled on the scows in this historical photograph is headed—to the bottom of Elliott Bay.

This was the quickest way to get rid of it, at more than 10,000 cubic yards a day. Here we see the final leg of the last of Denny Hill's 3,000-ft. journey to Elliott Bay. It came by an elevated conveyor belt down Battery St., out a 400-ft. viaduct, and then was piled onto double-sided barges. The barges were then towed offshore by tug and capsized 180 degrees, turning the top, bottom and vice versa. (Photographed from a tug, the scene shows one scow in tow and another behind it high in the water and being filled.)

At the time it did occur to some that this easy dumping was an awful waste of fill dirt. One daily newspaper, the habitually sensational *Seattle Star*, took up the campaign of halting, (as its front page banner headline for July 2, 1929 proclaimed), this "folly of wasting Denny Hill dirt." The *Star* revealed what everyone already knew. On its last leg, the Battery St. belt crossed over that "death trap Railroad Ave. [now Alaska Way] that needs several hundred thousand yards of the precious material for filling, so Seattle's doorstep will be a credit rather than a disgrace."

This disgraceful Railroad Ave. can be seen in our photograph below the white railing and above the mounds of Denny Hill dirt. The *Star*'s repeated calls to fill in between this timber trestle's worm-eaten pilings with the remains of the regrade came to nothing. Work on a seawall here did not begin until 1934, or four years after the last of Denny Hill was conveyed to the bottom of the bay.

In late 1928, after a 17 year hiatus, work began on leveling the last of Denny Hill. By then the city's engineers estimated that "Seattle had shoved probably 50 million cubic yards from the face of mother earth," and the total pile of regraded Seattle would reach 90 ft. higher than the Smith Tower with a pyramidic base a half-mile wide (now from the Kingdome to the library.)

On August 30, 1931 the *Times* reported "Wandering Denny Hill Won't Stay Put in Sound." The estimated final five million cubic feet of Denny Hill had pyramided high enough in Elliott Bay to become a hazard to shipping. A few days dredging reduced "the brow of the `new' Denny Hill to 44 ft. from the surface of the bay at low water."

Above The contemporary foot of Battery St. as seen from the Good-time Harbor Tour Boat. *Left* The Battery St. convenyor belt running west form 5th Ave.

Courtesy of Lawton Gowey

Courtesy of Lawton Gowey

Above One of the Denny Regrade hold-outs who refused to remove their house with the hill. *Below* This 1931 aerial shows most of the city's street-grid, from the 2nd Ave. Extension, lower right, to the fresh scar of the last Denny Regrade below the wing's tip. The 1929-30 regrade was begun just in time for the Great Depression, and the Seattle skyline did not change significantly from that time until the 1960s.

Below One of the last regrades self-righting scows dumps its load into Elliott Bay. *Right* the Dec. 1930 celebration of the last shovelfull.

Courtesy of Seattle Engineering Dept.

The making of the 5th Ave. cliff in 1910 with Denny School behind. The view looks north from Blanchard St.

Courtesy of Old Seattle Paperworks, Pike Place Market

56   Westlake

Both this "now" and "then" look north up Westlake Ave. from the southwest corner of Fourth Ave. and Pike St. Great things have been expected of this five-star hub since its creation in 1906 when the odd but bold intrusion of Westlake Ave. was at last cut through from Denny Way. (As of this writing, the city is still waiting.)

Our historical setting dates from 1909. All of the larger structures are new and seem to elegantly promise that this unique hub will develop into Seattle's 20th-century civic center. On the right is the Seaboard Building which now, with another five stories added, still fills that corner. Just beyond it is the American Hotel, and across Westlake, the Hotel Plaza. The flatiron Plaza stood there until 1931 when it was razed to the first floor level and rebuilt more modestly for Bartell Drugs which remained a tenant for over 50 years. During the prohibition years a cabaret in the Plaza's basement

was one of the town's more popular speakeasys.

In our historical scene the streets are only sparingly congested by a few horses, hacks, and three or four automobiles. The streetcars and people actually own the street, and the former are outfitted with cowcatchers to mercifully ensnare the latter. In 1909 if you stayed off the tracks (and stepped about what the horses left) you were usually free to safely jaywalk or even stand about and converse in the street—like the two men on the right of our scene.

To contemporary eyes the oddest feature of this cityscape is surely Fourth Ave.'s ascent up the southeast flank of Denny Hill. There is a grade difference of 85 feet between our "now" and "then" at Fourth's intersection with Virginia St.—a point we almost see on the photograph's far left. Within a year and a half this hill would be leveled to the non-descript elevation we are now used to.

Above Looking back at the intersection of 4th Ave. and Pike St.. *Below* The "now" scene was photographed in 1984—there have been some changes since then, but not to compare which was is planned for Westlake Mall.

Down Westlake in the 1930s.

An artist's early conception of Westlake and Fourth Avenues as routes for a city-wide system of elevated rapid transits.

The flatiron block Plaza Hotel during its and Westlake Avenue's 1906 construction. Fourth Ave., on the left, still rises to Denny Hill.*

But it is Westlake that is the centerpiece of this scene. If its sweeping line were continued on south through the central business district, it would at last meet First Ave. at Marion St. And that was the route for a Lake Union-bound boulevard proposed in 1876 by Seattle doctor and Mayor Gideon Weed.

Although the citizens disagreed with Weed's proposal, they were familiar with this part of the route for in 1872 a narrow-gauge railroad was cut through the forest here to carry coal from scows on Lake Union to bunkers at the foot of Pike St. The gondolas ran up this draw until 1878 when the route was abandoned for a new coal road to Newcastle that went around the south end of Lake Washington. Then this old railine, and future Westlake Ave., grew into a shrub-sided path popularly travelled for family picnics at Lake Union. It was then called "Down the Grade."

In 1882 a narrow boardwalk to the lake was built along the old line and David Denny's Western Mill first started Lake Union "working." By the late 1880s the sides of this little valley between Denny and Capitol hills were cleared; however, the streets which were cut across this gentle ravine did not conform to the lay of the land. The district of clapboard apartments and working-men's homes which developed here was one of Seattle's more obvious examples of the tendency of promoters' town plats to disregard the real topography.

In 1890 Luther Griffith, Seattle's young wizard of electric trolleys, realized this mistake in city planning. After buying up 53 lots along the old coal road's grade, he proposed to cut a multi-use boulevard through to Lake Union. The city council disagreed.

By the early 1900s the city's businesses had begun to move north out of Pioneer Square. Another and a new city center was desired, and the city engineers went back to the old Westlake proposals. The old route was surveyed in January 1905, and by November of the next year the 90-ft-wide street was paved and completed.

This was 30 years since Mayor Weed's original 1876 proposal. If this Westlake precedent holds true, then the Westlake Mall, which was first proposed in 1958 and has since been an frustration for five mayors—Clinton, Braman, Miller, Uhlman, and Royer—should be completed in 1988 to the glory of the re-elected fifth.

The foundation of the American Hotel was, obviously, sturdy enough to eventually support the full height of the Seaboard Bldg.

JUDKINS, CORNER SECOND AND COLUMBIA STREETS, SEATTLE, W. T.

Courtesy of University of Washington Historical Photography Collection

57 On the Shores of Wallingford

The photographer David Judkins and the lumberman J. R. McDonald both came to Seattle in 1883. This view of the train posing above the pile trestle on Lake Union's northern shore was photographed by Judkins in 1888 or 89. The name of the steam engine, painted on the coal bin at its rear, is the *J. R. McDonald*. In 1887 McDonald was named president of this railroad, the Seattle Lake Shore and Eastern.

Some of Judkins' work from the 1880s survived Seattle's great fire of 1889—probably because his studio was on a houseboat. Still most of his views are now lost, and the few that are not are mostly dog-eared and faded—or folded, like this one.

This is probably the oldest view of Lake Union shot from what is now part of Wallingford. The familiar ridge of Capitol Hill runs across the entire scene: close-to-town and clear-cut on the right, but still forested on the left. The darker firs in the middle distance on the left are on the peninsular tip of what is now Gasworks Park.

Judkins probably got off the train to take this portrait of it. He set his tripod a short distance east of the present intersection of Stone Way N. and N. Northlake Way. (The "now" shot is in line with Judkins' but was photographed from a position that is near the end of Judkins' train and so considerably closer to Gas Works Park on the left.)

In Judkins' scene, passengers are leaning out of the windows and doors, and from between the cars, and that may be the fireman posing atop the engine's cowcatcher. The train is pointed towards Seattle, and is possibly returning from its popular Sunday excursion run to Snoqualmie Falls. The *Seattle Illustrated*, published in 1890, described this journey as "widely celebrated and one of the frequent pleasure trips of the Seattleites."

Perhaps S.L.S.& E. president McDonald arranged with Judkins to have this photo taken of his railroad and his

Lake Union Police Dock next to Gasworks Park, on the left.

namesake engine. The January 1890 issue of *West Shore* magazine, in an article entitled "A Typical Man of Business," featured McDonald as a northwestern paragon of how "brains, energy, and enterprise had made for the wonderful development of the West."

SNOQUALMIE FALLS, KING CO. WASH.

But it really wasn't McDonald's engine or his railroad. One month after the *West Shore*'s praise, McDonald resigned his presidency and sued the S.L.S.& E. for the $6,000 annual salary he claimed was owed him. McDonald had been a regional figurehead for a company financed with eastern capital and managed by easterners. No longer needed, he returned to his lumber, and his name was retired from the S.L.S.& E.'s rolling stock.

Courtesy of Seattle Public Library

An excursion party on the S.L.S.E.RR—probably to Snoqualmie Falls—poses at the rear of a coach.

The Casey Jones Special heading out of the old Seattle Lakeshore & Eastern Railroad right-of-way along the northern shore of Lake Union—now the Burke Gilman bike trail. Behind are a remnant of the part of the old gasworks that was not kept.

Courtesy of Lawton Gowey

58   Fremont Bridge

Northend motorists are by now very familiar with this contemporary view of the Fremont Bridge, for when it's up— which it has been more than a half-million times since it started teeter-tottering 68 years ago—there's three or more minutes to gaze up at it and beyond to the green skyline of Fremont.

The bascule bridge was built for the Lake Washington Ship Canal and opened, when the canal did, in 1917. The older photo and bridge was shot about 14 years before that. The scene was first published in the June issue of *Pacific Northwest*, a short-lived but slick month-ly whose primary purpose was to promote Seattle's culture and real estate by putting the best construction on everything.

Fremont was no exception. The *Pacific Northwest* editors emphasized that it was near the "geographical center" of Seattle. And it was, but only because, when the new little town was incorporated into the city in 1891, Seattle's northern city limits were stretched into the forest wilderness beyond Green Lake. Thus, Fremont found itself both in the center of the city and yet far from it.

Sitting at the Northwest corner of

Lake Union, Fremont had to be. At the outlet of the lake, it was an obvious site for a bridge, a lumber mill, built in 1888, and a town, platted that year by a couple entrepreneurs from Fremont, Nebraska. The Seattle Lake Shore & Eastern R.R. came through there a year earlier, and by 1890 electric trolleys were speeding at 20 miles per hour above a timber trestle along the western shore of the lake giving a fast ride to and from Seattle "proper."

In the older photo we can see the trolleys and tracks running across the old Fremont bridge. Although we cannot see the outlet, there is evidence of its north bank just this side of the Fremont mill. In 1902 this stream had been straightened and widened all the way to Ballard. The January 30, 1903 *Post-Intelligencer* reported that now "the capacity is at least three times as great as that of the natural ditch which was previously the only source of the outlet for Lake Union."

After the 1903 washout the city engineers raised the Fremont Bridge to the grade of Fremont's 34th Ave. That put the old Westlake Blvd storefronts on the Queen Anne side of the bridge (right of center) one story below the new grade. In 1914 this elevated bridge met a similar fate when once again the Fremont Dam broke.

NORTH VIEW. N 34TH & FREMONT AVE 8-28-23 5.20 A.M

OUT BOUND

Courtesy of Seattle Engineering Dept.

The improved ditch and dam at the outlet were designed to control the sending of logs downstream to the dozen or so mills at Ballard. The dam was also meant to control floods, but within the year it broke and almost flooded Fremont, which in 1903 was still a dry town being within the four-mile circle of sobriety which then surrounded the University of Washington and protected the temperance of its students and neighbors. Later, when this circle was cut in half, Fremont got wet with more than its share of taverns. But in 1903, the *Pacific Northwest* article promised that it was "entirely free of saloons and promises ever to be. The suburb is composed of the very best citizens in the West."

Actually, it still has them. Today Fremont is one of Seattle's model neighborhoods for good-natured activism, and the bartenders and Baptists work side-by-side. This neighborly concern has issued in, among other things: the Fremont Fair, one of the area's first foodbanks, the Fremont Public Association, and the monthly free newspaper, the *Forum*, expanded in 1986 to *The North Seattle Press.*

Inside the *Forum*'s 1985 *Official Visitors Guide to Fremont*, this landmark town is wonderfully displayed. Included is a fine short history of Fremont and an article on its bascule titled "The Busiest Drawbridge on the Planet Earth." These wonderfully balanced machines are a kind of test of faith. For the motorist in a hurry, they are a bit of purgatory. But for those in grace, this repeated and relaxed drawing of the Fremont Bridge may be an intimation of a heaven filled with bascule bridges performing for the souls of those confirmed in Fremont.

Left All three of these scenes are Seattle Engineering Dept. records of the Fremont Bridge in the early 1920s.

Only about 15 years seperates these two views of Fremont from Queen Anne Hill. The older scene, above, dates from about 1890, or within a year or two of Fremont's founding. In the bottom scene, the elevated Fremont bridge is under construction.

Courtesy of Seattle Engineering Dept.

59 Bridging the Gap

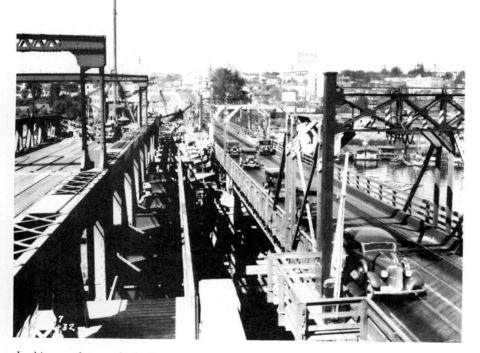

Looking north towards the district between the two bridges.

The northeast corner of Lake Union, where it narrows into Portage Bay, has been spanned by five bridges. In this historical view we see bridge No. 3, a temporary two-lane wood trestle. For one year only, it diverted traffic while the old worn-out wooden Eastlake bridge (bridge No. 2) was rebuilt and widened into the steel and concrete bascule University bridge we still use today—and see in the "now" scene.

On May 22, 1932 the *Seattle Times* reported, "All streetcars now using the University Bridge will be re-routed tomorrow morning over the nearby temporary trestle while the main structure is undergoing alteration." At 4:15 the next morning, the bridge's tender pulled the switch to lower the single jack-knife span. Nothing happened! During the night someone—guesses were a disgruntled worker, an aggravated landowner, or harassed houseboater—had climbed the bridge's supports, stolen the fuses, and jammed the door to the machinery room. The problem took less than two hours to correct; meanwhile the commuters went walking.

The temporary span was built primarily for the use of the city's streetcars. Motorists were strongly urged to use other bridges. Traffic controllers warned that here automobiles "will have to follow and precede streetcars" at a safe distance. Motorists soon discovered that it was hard for authorities to control their access to the bridge and so began using the temporary bridge freely. So freely, in fact, that at the April 7, 1933 dedication of the new six-lane University Bridge (bridge No. 4, still with us), Seattle Mayor Dore noted that, through its one-year service, the retiring timber bridge had handled more autos than either the Fremont, Aurora, or Montlake bridges.

Bridge No. 4 was formally opened when Franklin Roosevelt, performing another electric inaugural from the White House, pressed a golden key which sounded a fire siren on the bridge and released a huge flag above the bridge's center bascule. The University band struck up the "Stars and Stripes," as a squadron of Boeing planes droned overhead. "The staccato chatter of motor boats" was added from below.

Below While the wood approaches to the University Bridge were replaced by steel and concrete, a congested temporary two-lane timber-pile span took its place.

Courtesy of Seattle Engineering Dept.

In its first 24 hours, 37,794 vehicles passed over the new University Bridge. This meant that G. M. Ownes of Wallingford who guessed 37,793, and Robert Sheehand of the University District who guessed 37,795 each got $325 worth of script good in district stores as winners in the University Retailers Association's "Bridge Guessers Contest." (The average daily count for vehicular crossings in 1983 was 27,735. Bridge No. 5, the freeway bridge, has a lot to do with the lower count.)

Bridge No. 1 was the little Latona Bridge dedicated July 1, 1891. It was built across the channel in the same direction as bridge No. 5—which we can see arching across the top of our contemporary photo.

Courtesy of Seattle Public Library

Top the old Latona Bridge in its last days as seen from the University Bridge which in its initial construction is seen *below* with the University District behind.

Courtesy of Seattle Engineering Dept.

60 UniverCity

UniverCity author Roy Neilsen poses, 61 years later, near the matinee line-up for the "Gang" comedy.

In 1925 the University District tried to change its name. It had become such a metropolitan neighborhood that it promoted itself as "UniverCity." The name didn't catch on but the district itself did. One large addition that year was the University Book Store which moved out of its basement rooms in the old Meany Hall and onto University Way. At the time this move off campus was expected to be temporary, but business on the "Ave" proved so good the bookstore stayed put.

Another evidence of this cultural vigor was district resident and promoter T. L. Murphey's decision to clear a few front yards and houses, including his own, on University Way north of 45th St. and erect a showpiece 1,300-seat theater.

The two historical photos here show Murphy's home (behind the car) and the Egyptian Theater which took its place, opening on Christmas Day, 1925. Here the theater is two years old. The license plates on the autos parked below its marquee reveal the 1927 date.

Both these historical scenes are included in a new book, *UniverCity: The Story of the University District in Seattle*. The author, Roy Neilsen, stands in the street in the "now" scene a few feet and almost 60 years from where the matinee line of Gang comedy fans wait beside what is now the north door to Pay 'N Save Drugs. The commercial urge which replaced the theater with the drugstore in 1960 also unfortunately covered the building's original delicate details with an undecorated modern facade. This conversion also replaced the theater's charming chain-supported marquee with the drug store's plastic sign.

In 1936, or one year before Roy Neilsen graduated from the University of Washington, the district branch of Pacific National Bank started collecting District photos through contests and other promotions. Roy Neilsen eventually became the manager of that bank, and now nine years retired, he returns a part of that collection to his neighbors through his book.

Above The T.L.Murphy residence at the future site of the Egyptian Theatre.
Below The University Book Store—most of its sign is showing above trolley #511—moved out of Denny Hall and onto "The Ave" in 1925.

61 The "Soul of the University"

In the autumn of 1933, the University of Washington Board of Regents named the school's library after former University President Henry Suzzallo who had just died. Seven years earlier, in the winter of 1927, when the library was first opened to students, one of them named it the "Cathedral of Books."

The name was appropriate not only for the building's Gothic lines, but also for the spiritual priorities that were put into its design. President Suzzallo explained the need for a new library with the observation, "The library is the soul of the University."

With this admonition, the library's architects, Bebb and Gould, designed a cathedral which was less for books than for looking up from books. Seventy-three feet above, its decorated Tudor vaults invited erudite gazing. It was one of the most edifying study halls this side of Oxford. The *Seattle Times* reported, "It is pronounced by experts to be the most beautiful reading room on the continent, and is ranked among the most beautiful in the world." Lit by the pensive light of 36-ft-high stained glass windows, 240-ft-long with a quiet floor of compressed cork, only the outer walls below the windows were lined with bookshelves. The room itself seemed to promise wisdom. It was a significant space that was the cen-

ter of the University's soul.

A decade before it was named after him, the university's library was identified with Henry Suzzallo. The man who would eventually fire Suzzallo, Governor Roland Hartley, characterized the proposed library as "Suzzallo's extravagance." Hartley who liked neither intellectuals nor the university tried to withhold all tax support from the school. When a Suzzallo-led lobby overrode the governor's veto, he was so enraged that after attacking Suzzallo's nationality, his salary of $18,000 a year, and his library, he had him sacked by a specially-appointed board of regents.

In 1932 Hartley, failing re-election, was sacked by the voters, and one year later Suzzallo's name was put above the door of his soulful extravagance.

In the historical setting the Suzzallo library stands magnificently alone. We see it through a screen of poplars whose shadows repeat the line of the paths that cross the spacious lawn. The soft service of that lawn is still remembered by a few hundred thousand alumni who rested upon it.

In 1969 a big hole was dug here and the results are both seen and unseen in the contemporary scene. Below and hid-

The scene up through the center of the "Red Square" exhaust towers.

den is a 1000-car garage whose considerable monoxide fumes are drawn out through a 140-ft smokestack disguised as a brick monolith. Here it casts its shadow on the library.

Above, where there was grass, is now the red-tiled expanse officially named the Suzzallo Quadrangle, but almost always called Red Square. This popular name was probably inevitable, but its choice was helped along by the 1969 University *Daily* news editor, Cassandra Amesely. Given a class assignment in propaganda, she decided, "My project would be to get the students to refer to it as Red Square." And so, she managed both the news and the name.

Whether fronted by green grass or red tile, Suzzallo's "Cathedral of Books" still has its big room inside, and there one can still look up from a good or boring book and visualize the soul of the university 73 feet up.

Courtesy of Old Seattle Paperworks, Pike Place Market

The proposed plan for the University's library, was considerably more elaborate than the final result. However, the spacious reading room *right* was ready in 1927.

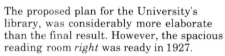

62 Greenlake Panorama

Hidden, but not lost, in the files of the Green Lake Library are the 16 pages of *The Green Lake News: Anniversary Number.* On November 26, 1903 the *News* was one year old and excited at having survived to record and promote the suburb's "amazing growth."

The anniversary number includes a wide-angle photograph of this booming neighborhood captioned "Birdseye View of Green Lake, taken in 1903." It is a composite of three negatives photographed—probably on commission from the newspaper—by Asahel Curtis. (Curtis' 1903 panorama is reproduced here; however, it's too wide to run continuously, so only the most southerly third is printed below the center panel.

In 1903 Green Lake was in the midst of its second spurt. John Martin, one of its boomers, confessed in the pages of the anniversary number, "A little more than three years ago an irrepressible desire for freedom from the noisy traffic of the city forced the writer into a search for a quiet home...The attractiveness of

Green Lake was irresistible. Then not more than 500 people surrounded it. Now there are nearly 10,000!" Martin was not complaining. Three years earlier he had purchased 20 Green Lake lots.

Martin claimed that this flight to the suburban lake was caused by the congested city, effective advertising (like his own), and what he called the "two-mile charmed circle." This referred to the liquor-free zone which radiated from the University of Washington and "within which by the grace of the legislature, no saloon can come."

The first boom was in the early 1890s when settler-promoters like W. D. Wood, F. A. McDonald, and Guy Phinney bought up big chunks of forest about the lake, cleared and platted some of it, and constructed the Greenlake Circle Railroad Loop around the lake and up from Fremont. (This Green Lake era is shown in the second panorama printed here.) The international crash of 1893 stopped the land rush and slowed the trolleys.

Phinney's land is now Woodland Park. We can see its uncut verdure on the center panel's far left. And the ridge that runs across the photograph (just under the snowy Olympics) still bears his name.

McDonald's parcel was to the southeast, much of it now included in Wallingford, (left panel printed below-left.) Wood's property covers much of the panorama's center in east Green Lake.

Wood was the visionary (and one-time Seattle mayor) who for years pleaded—to quote him from the Anniversary Issue—that "the Green Lake frontage be secured by the city for park purposes, and that the lake be made a water park upon the plan that has made Minneapolis so famous."

Wood was convincing. The city soon purchased the lake, and in 1911 lowered it seven feet, thereby exposing hundreds of acres for park use. The largest part of this reclamation was the bay that used to dip into east Green Lake and which is now the large playfield across from the Green Lake shopping district.

The one landmark that survived almost into the present is the Green Lake Public School on the far left of the center panel. It was first opened to students in September of 1903—or within a few weeks of Curtis' recording it. The wooden school, closed in 1983 by the fire marshal, was designated a landmark in 1981 by the city's Landmarks Preservation Board. This did not prevent it from being razed, however, in the summer of 1986.

Courtesy of Seattle Public Library

East Greenlake stump-pulling in the early 1890s. Phinney Ridge is in the distance.

What is now the Greenlake Playfield was once the East Greenlake bay. Here, right, we see the dike traversing the bay in 1913, behind which the bay was both drained and filled-in. The view looks north towards the still open Green Lake Public Library. The mid-1890s panorama that runs across both pages shows another part of the northeast shore.

Courtesy of Old Seattle Paperworks, Pike Place Market

63 "Where the Dollar Works Overtime"

When Charles Gerrish and his younger brother Arthur opened their first of eventually 15 grocery stores on January 19, 1903 in Green Lake's eastside neighborhood, they hung over the door a modest sign which read simply, "Gerrish Bros. Grocers." Soon the *Green Lake News* reported, "several people dropped into the unpretentious place and were instantly struck by the noticeable economy of space, the neatness of the interior."

The neat shop prospered. That first winter month they grossed exactly $421.46. Only ten months later they took in $3,146.38, and by the end of their first year they moved into a new two-story clapboard built to their prescriptions on Woodlawn Ave. N.E., one block north of N.E. 72 St.

This tidy scene of the second store's interior shows that they moved their "neat economy" with them. But this nifty place has grown a few pretensions—like the pyramids of soap boxes, the fan of brooms, and the can-constructed icons that are a satisfying use of

Looking east on NE 72nd St. from Green Lake Way.

all that open space beneath the high ceiling.

And the store's exterior was downright boistrous. It took the entire 2-1/2-story facade to broadcast that this was "THE CASH STORE, WHERE THE DOLLAR WORKS OVERTIME...It Pays To Buy For CASH...Paying Cash Makes No Enemies...Orders Over $3 Delivered."

On the open shelves waiting for pick-up or delivery were many brands we're still familiar with, like Hills Bros. and Heinz. But others like Fairbanks Gold Dust Washing Powder and Sunny Monday soap have slipped down the drain of history—victims, perhaps, of one of those many detergent wars that clean the decades of too much washing powder.

This, obviously, was not a supermarket. Here you asked the clerk, and there were plenty of them. The Gerrish brothers' sister Clara is on the right behind the bulk goods. Next in line is the younger brother Arthur, and clerk Kelly. The man in hat and vest, with his back to the sanitary glass cabinets filled with baked goods and his hand on the cooler, is unidentified. But the clerk on the right is Earl Blanchard, who eventually bought this Green Lake store from the brothers when they moved on to one of their many others.

The founder, Charles Gerrish, is not in this picture, but the identifications were made by his son Charles Jr. who sits beside the organ in the contemporary photo.

From the older photo Charles Jr. remembers best the glass confectionary in the left foreground. It is a bitter-sweet memory. Here in 1910, not long after this photo was taken, his mother took

The most recent occupant of 7206 Woodlawn NE is Cox Music. Jerry vander Pol, organist and owner, stands next to Charles Gerrish Jr.

the 4-year-old to this glass counter and told him. "You can have anything you want." It was the last he remembers of his mother, who died soon after at the age of 24 of complications in surgery.

By the age of 15 Charles Jr. was out on his own working in theaters, restaurants, and, of course, grocery stores. When, as he calls them, the "dirty thirties" hit, his father loaned him 500 solid non-inflated depression-time dollars to start his own store.

Unlike the Gerrish Brothers who moved around a lot through their many northend stores, the grocer Charles Gerrish Jr. stayed put in one Queen Anne neighborhood for 42 years. When he retired from his Quality Market on McGraw St. in 1980, Charles Jr. was 75 years old. Now at 80 he's in active retirement, out almost every day visiting old friends and making new ones. He's tall and handsome and has hands big enough to hide a cantaloupe.

Courtesy of Lawton Gowey

64   A New Way to Ballard

Car #108 preparing to leave the City-County Bldg for its inaugural run to Ballard.

As its destination sign indicates, car No. 108 was "special." At 2:30 on the Sunday afternoon of January 27, 1918 "to the music of the Police Department band tooting in competition with the cheers of 200 people," it began the fledgling Seattle Municipal Railways' inaugural run to Ballard. The *Seattle Star* reported: "Four cent street car service from the heart of Seattle to Ballard! It's a reality today, folks...in up-to-date cars operated by smiling crews...and financed by the plain people of Seattle who put up the money and bought the bonds."

On board, besides the Police band and the *Star* reporter, were Mayor Hi Gill, the city council, and an entourage of bureaucrats including the street department's photographer. The parade of leading streetcar and many trailing motorcars stopped once on the 25-minute inaugural ride to Ballard, and once again on the return trip to City Hall.

Both were scheduled interruptions for the official photographer to record Seattle's (and so also Ballard's) new city-

Below The Ballard Booster Club's Sunday ceremony on Ballard's Market Street. Both the Carnegie Library, far right, and the theatre, right center, have been preserved, although the theatre's name has changed as has its facade.

owned streetcar on its then brand-new Ballard Bridge. The historical scene is from the second stop—on the ride back home. Many of what the *Star* reporter counted as the "dozens of autos and hundreds of men and women which were waiting for the car when it [first] passed over the bridge" are still there to admire it on its return crossing. Car No. 108's motorman Dettler and its conductor Johnston pose at the front window, but neither of them is smiling. Nor is anyone else.

Moments earlier the serious political purpose of all this was explained to a crowd of over 1,000 at a celebration staged by the Ballard Booster Club on Ballard's Market Street. Mayor Gill exclaimed, "This occasion marks your emancipation from the financial interests that have fought municipal ownership and operation of cars." The City's Corporation Council added that it was also "A warning! If utility corporations won't live up to their obligations, the people will own and operate all utilities."

Within the year, Seattle did acquire, at an inflated price, the rest of the city's privately owned and mostly dilapidated trolley lines. Today, of course, Metro's common carriers are still running over Ballard's bridge as part of a transit system which in 1984 was the first public bus system to receive the American Public Transit Association's prestigious Outstanding Achievement Award.

It's not possible to determine whether the driver of Metro bus No. 1276 is smiling.

Right Ballard's Carnegie Library when it was still a library.

Courtesy of Lawton Gowey

Courtesy of Seattle Public Library

65 From Magnolia to Ballard

It was, no doubt, to record the full breadth of bustling Ballard that Asahel Curtis lugged his camera up the steep side of Magnolia's northeast face for this birdseye view across Salmon Bay. The scene's rough foreground was probably of less interest to him.

In 1905 the Federal Bureau of Statistics described Ballard as "A hustling center of activity...with exceptional manufacturing advantages." Actually, Ballard was then more than exceptional; it was downright superlative. And the bureau had the statistics to prove it. The 1905 production record of 828,500,000 shingles meant Ballard remained the "shingle capital of the world."

Most of those shingles were handled at least once by Scandinavian men, many of whom would have rather been fishing or farming. But Ballard's mills were

where most of the work was, and we can see a few of them here on the then still salt water shores of Salmon Bay.

Also showing, on the right, are the two bridges to Ballard. The further and straighter one was the notoriously shaky route for streetcars and traffic. The curving and closer timber-trestle was the Great Northern R.R.'s main line which then still passed directly through the backyards of Ballard's dozen-plus sawmills. (When the Ballard Locks were built in the mid-teens the railroad was diverted west of the locks to the bascule bridge it still crosses today.)

The dark line of the Curtis horizon extends left from a stand of the original Woodland Park virgin firs (on the right) through a forest borderline that is now the cleared neighborhoods of Greenwood and Crown Hill. Closer to the camera on the brushy Magnolia side of Salmon Bay, there is as yet no Fisherman's Terminal.

But, I confess, it is the rugged Magnolia foreground of the photograph that first lured me to it and eventually sent me on a search for Asahel Curtis' original perch.

First, for orientation, I climbed to the top of the steep steps at the summit of Dravus Street. Almost at once, I felt the thrill of discovery for surviving just below me was the familiar barnlike roof of the prominent white house in the left foreground of the Curtis scene.

In another instant I was knocking at the front door of 3231 26th Ave. W. Lloyd Nelson opened it and invited me into a front room decorated with guitars and woodland tapestries. Nelson explained that when he moved into his home-with-a-view in 1959, it was a half century old. A quick check of the county assessor's records proved him right. This house on lots 9 and 10 of block 4 of the Pullman Addition was constructed in 1904 by H. J. Linse. Nelson is the home's fifth owner, at least, since Linse.

Helping with the research, Nelson took the Curtis photo to his neighbors and determined that the house just north of his (towards Ballard) was built in 1905. Since his neighbor's home is not in the historical photo, we can conclude that Curtis shot this scene either in late 1904 or early 1905.

Ballard in 1905 had ten schools, 59 teachers, 2,850 students, and the Bureau of Statistics estimated the population to be 13,000 with over 828 million shingles.

Courtesy of Old Seattle Paperworks, Pike Place Market

In 1912 the Port of Seattle bought this Salmon Bay site for its planned Fisherman's Terminal. This 1915 view looks across part of the site and Salmon Bay to Ballard's Seattle Cedar Mill.

Lloyd Nelson, a retired forklift operator and "full-blooded Swede," did not work in the Ballard mills but did play his guitars in the Ballard bars with his 3-piece band, the Harvesters. Since leaving 21 years of forklifting at American Can Co. in 1976, Nelson has divided his time between operating a lawn service, driving his camper to the region's lakes, and occasionally, "for my own pleasure," picking his guitar.

So we can conclude that as a landscaper, sportsman, and musician, Lloyd Nelson is one Scandinavian who managed to get back into fishing and farming.

Bill Burden

Lloyd Nelson at home.

66 On the Road to Lake Forest Park

Although it's impossible to tell from the photographs, these historical and contemporary shots were taken within 100 yards and 73 years of each other.

Roads were important to Hanson, and if you look at a map of Lake Forest Park (or drive around in it), you can tell why. Hanson proclaimed that his new community was "the only large subdivision in the Northwest that has been platted entirely to contour." Unlike Seattle, which Hanson said "was never built, it just grew" in the "insane and idiotic gridiron fashion," Lake Forest Park, "before a home was built," was laid out with boulevards that ran "according to the contour of the ground. No straight lines are tolerated." Knolls and hills "will not be ruthlessly destroyed by the Seattle leveling madness."

And the Seattle of 1912 was a mess—dirty and tired from years of moving its hills around, and its exploding population in. Developments like Lake Forest Park and the roads to them like the Bothell highway were more than the latter-day escapes to suburbia; they were returns to nature.

The photos were probably also used by future Seattle mayor Ole Hanson who, in 1912, was just beginning to promote his Lake Forest Park Addition. Included in Barbara Bender's mammoth 488-page history, *Growing Up With Lake Forest Park* are examples of Hanson's advertising copy. First, for promotional reasons, he changed the name of Bothell Way to Lake Forest Boulevard.

The contemporary scene was photographed from the top of a trash can at the southern corner of the Lake Forest Park shopping center. The view looks across Bothell Way to the north entrance of Sheridan Beach. Now on a warm weekend almost as many bicycles pass by here on the Burke Gilman Trail as autos cross this intersection where Bothell Way concludes its long descent down from Lake City.

The historical photo was shot from a little way south and up the hill from here. In the distance the still-wild ridges of (right to left) Sheridan Heights, Cedar Park, Chelsea and View Ridge, and the Sandpoint flats identify Lake Washington's northwestern shoreline like a fingerprint.

On the left, the poles closest to the water mark the right-of-way of the Seattle Lake Shore & Eastern Railroad—now the line of the bike trail. The railroad was cut through here in late 1887, or about 21 years before Gerhard Erickson, the "good roads politician" from Bothell, managed to convince the state legislature to actually pay for state roads—including this one which in its first and crudest condition was named after him.

When its surface was hardened, Erickson Road was given the heroic name "Victory Highway," and when it reached Everett in the summer of 1912, it was called proudly the "Pacific Highway." It was, however, still not the fastest way to get to Everett. That took an hour on board the electric Everett Interurban Railway, completed north in 1910. (You'll find more on that in the Echo Lake story.)

The historical photo is but one of a set taken by the photographers Webster & Stevens in late 1912 or early 1913 to show off the improved Pacific Highway. For those who could afford an auto, the weekend excursion to Bothell was a favorite recreation, although almost always punctuated by blow-outs. Many drivers kept elaborate miles-and-minute logs which scientifically recorded every event enroute including the frequent flats which were then still part of the adventure or test of automotive manhood. Those without cars or who could not hitch a ride could still enjoy the pictures.

Courtesy of Old Seattle Paperworks, Pike Place Market

Courtesy of Old Seattle Paperworks, Pike Place Market

67 Sammamish Slough

There is a long curve on Bothell Way that takes motorists through an almost 180-degree hairpin swoop before they arrive in downtown Bothell. It is called the Wayne Curve, and for almost 75 years this paved oddity has been a local landmark, because drivers don't forget it.

But before that highway, there were two other "ways" to get around Wayne Curve. We can see them intersect in this historical photograph where the Sammamish Slough passes beneath the railroad trestle. Although the bridge has been changed, the slough is the same—almost.

The Sammamish Slough is now the 10 miles of dredged ditch which connects lakes Sammamish and Washington. Once it was almost twice as long as it meandered through marshes, under snares, and around sandbars. Now one of the last of its original curves is here at Wayne.

When coal was discovered at Issaquah in the 1860s, it was sometimes shipped on scows up Lake Sammamish, and then driven on by poles down Squak

Slough (its original name and also the title of a book by Amy Stickney and Lucille McDonald. Much of this writing is based on theirs.) Unless the river was flooding, the normal passage for poling coal was a week on the slough.

The few settlers that entered the valley during the 1870s used dug-outs and rowboats. Between the time the Woodin family moved into Woodinville in 1871, and the Bothell family into Bothell in 1884, only a few score more pioneers established claims along the Squak.

One of the first, in 1872, was an Englishman named John Blyth who settled here at Wayne Curve, about two miles upstream from Lake Washington. Here he lived a lonely bachelor life until 1885 when he married Christina Bargquist, his neighbor's sister, only three months after she arrived from Sweden. The language barrier was easily broken by a cooperation of romance and pioneer necessity.

John Blyth built his home between the river and what in 1887 became the Seattle Lake Shore and Eastern Railroad's right-of-way. From the start, the railroad put the valley to work pushing com-

Another picnic scene, this one on Lake Washington. *Below* Polling a dugout across a fallen tree—a pioneer necessity for reaching into the forest of the Puget Sound basin.

Sammamish River
Route of Steamer City of Bothel

Courtesy of Michael Maslan

This view of the Wayne Curve railroad bridge was photographed by Lucy Campbell Coe. She is featured in story 24 First Hill Home.

merce, including the Blyths' who provided board for the crews as they built the trestle across the slough. With their earnings, Christina and John built an addition to their farm house for their growing family.

But while giving work, the railroad also took it away. With its coming, the shallow-draft lake steamers, with names like the *Arrow*, *Duck Hunter*, *May Blossom*, *Squak*, and *City of Bothell*, that ventured into the slough were not as in demand for moving produce, passengers, and duck hunters. And, where the rails crossed the water (in our picture), an indignity was added when the steamer City of Bothell had to unhinge its stack to pass under.

The slough suffered its greatest revisions in 1916 when the Army Corps of Engineers lowered Lake Washington nine feet and straightened much of the river.

That was the end of steaming up the slough. By then, also, a red brick Pacific Highway was horseshoeing around Wayne Curve on its slippery way to Everett by way of Bothell. One can still - drive on the last of those bricks by turning off Bothell Way at the golf course just before the Wayne Curve.

John Blyth died in 1901, but Christina lived on to see much of their farm carpeted into the Wayne Golf Course in 1931. In the mid-1950s their son Joseph sold 11 acres more to the Bothell Lions Club who in 1959 donated it as a park to the city of Bothell.

It is from Blyth Park that the contemporary view of the trestle was shot. The Wayne Curve is the same, although the river is lowered. And so, obviously, is the proper attire for a picnic on Squak Slough.

BOTHELL, WASH.

68 Bucolic Bothell

The older view across Sammamish Slough looks towards the bucolic side of early-century Bothell. The year is 1908 or 9. In 1908 the Lake Washington steamer *May Blossom* was launched from Pete LaPointe's shipyard at Leschi Park to begin its regular service from Seattle to Bothell landing, and mid-points along the lake and and the slough.

Here the tourists, or as they were called by the crew the "rubberneckers," aboard her have cows to their starboard side and Alfred Pearson's barn and freshly mowed field to their port side. Bucolic, indeed.

The Swedish immigrant Pearson took his 40 acres on this hill in 1883. (Considering traditional Scandinavian rivalries, that was surely a few years before it became regularly known as Norway Hill.) Two years later David Bothell and family settled across the

CITY OF BOTHELL

Author Jim Faber, caught, somewhat candidly, at the Puget Sound Maritime Historical Society's MOHAI exhibit based on Faber's book, *Steamer's Wake.*

the Pacific Highway was completed through Bothell as far as Everett, and the call for steamer service up the lake to Bothell Landing was suddenly superannuated by the slippery thrill of racing over the new red brick highway.

And by then the No. 3 *City of Bothell* had been pulled from the slough and sold to the Anderson Steamboat Co. Capt. John Anderson soon renamed her the *Swan* and steamed her off the lake through the tricky Black River escape to Puget Sound. After a few years of taxing across the Port Washington narrows between Manette and Bremerton, the *May Blossum-City of Bothell-Swan* burned to the water in 1917, at the tender age of nine. And for a few years more she lay as a derelict in Dye inlet.

In the wet winter months this green summer scene between Bothell and Norway Hill was usually flooded and sometimes frozen. Then the citizens of Bothell (and their looser cows) could skate over to the Pearson's place.

But now the slough is both much lower and more regular. Soon after Lake Washington was dropped nine feet in 1916 for the opening of this fresh water harbor to the ship canal, the Army Corps of Engineers reshaped the river.

The wider-angled contemporary winter view looks from Bothell across a dredged and ditch-shaped Sammamish Slough, being worked here by two black bird dogs, not cows. Beyond, hidden beneath trees and snug in their expensive homes, not barns, are Italians, Germans, and, perhaps, even Estonians living in suburban harmony with Danes and Swedes on Norway Hill.

slough from Pearson and in 1888 platted Bothell, or the side of this scene behind the photographer.

In 1908 Bothell was still a town small enough to let a few of its citizens' milchcows freely replenish their cuds by the riverside. But Captain Cox and the Bothell Transportation Co.'s other owners took a less pastoral view of their town and soon renamed this flower of their small fleet, the *May Blossom*, the *City of Bothell.*

This was a progressive habit of theirs. This was the third *City of Bothell*—each one bigger than its predecessor. But this was their last. By 1912

Courtesy of Michael Maslan

Bothell from Norway Hill.

NEAR BOTHEL?

Somewhere on the slough.

69   Echo Lake and the Everett Interurban

It took an average of one hour and five rapid-transit minutes for the Seattle-Everett Interurban to pass between the two cities. The electric cars could reach 60 m.p.h. on straight stretches—an adventure still remembered by many. It ceased running only 47 years ago.

The interurban stopped at North Park, Pershing, Foy, Richmond Highlands, Alderwood, Ronald, and several lakeside stations, as well, including: Martha, Silver, Ballinger, Bitter, and Echo lakes.

The name "Bitter" was misleading for that lake was the spot for the decidedly sweet excitement of Playland, for many years the region's largest amusement park. I still remember that roller-coaster. But few will remember Echo Lake as it appears in this scene's historical setting.

Construction started on the Interurban in 1902. Beginning in Ballard, by 1905 it reached 14 miles out to Lake Ballinger, just beyond Echo Lake. The line prospered, at first, not so much from paying customers as by hauling lumber and its by-products. The forest wilderness it cut through, it also helped cut down.

It's a fair speculation that Fred Sander, the interurban's builder, hired Asahel Curtis, the photographer, to shoot this morning view of the new-looking pile trestle that spanned the swampy northeast corner of Echo Lake shortly after it was built in 1904 or 5.

Sander soon sold out to the streetcar monopolists, Stone & Webster. By 1910 they completed the line to Everett and replaced Sander's little pasenger cars (like the one posing on the trestle) with ten long and plush air-conditioned common carriers. In 1912 the company also buried its Echo Lake wood trestle beneath a landfill.

Next year, 1913, Herman Butzke, his wife, and daughter Florence moved into a two-room cabin they built at the southwest corner—the opposite shore from Curtis' shot—of Echo Lake. They were the third family on the lake, and Florence Butzke Erickson still lives there. During the summer of 1917 nurses and doctors from the new and nearby Firlands Sanitarium periodically escaped from their care for the tubercular to swim in the clear waters of Echo Lake. With their help, Butzke built a few lakeside dressing rooms, and thereby began the half century of the Echo Lake Bathing Beach. (It closed in 1966 for the construction of condos.)

The Seattle-Everett Interurban did not last so long, but when it did quit, it was one of the last of the nation's rapid transits to surrender to the trackless automobile.

On February 20, 1939, two thousand well-wishers gathered with a 50-piece band at the Everett station for the last send-off. Underway, the passengers, most of them members of the Everett Young Mens Business Club, sang Auld Lang Syne, and, all along the line, handkerchief-waving groups met them at every crossing, some illuminated and warmed by bonfires. Reaching Seattle the *Post Intelligencer* reported, "The Everett club men detrained, and climbed into two large brilliantly lighted special buses. They went back the modern way."

This "modern way" was, of course, the Pacific Coast Highway or, in town, Aurora Avenue. It, like the interurban

Both views *above* show the Seattle-Everett Interurban in her last days. In the *top* scene the northbound Car 55 crosses Highway 99. Then Aurora had to jog under this bridge which in this way was a practical symbol of the dominance the railway would only finally relinguish in 1939 to the automobile and a straightened highway. Harold Hill took this photo in 1939, the Interurban's last year. Hill also shot the above photo, again, of Car 55 —this time southbound at 105th and Evanston.

also passed by Echo Lake, and in the late 1920s when it was being built, lots beside the lake were being pushed as the "highlight of Plateau Norte: the most beautiful and attractive homesite addition ever offered. A heavily traveled highway such as the new Seattle-Everett hundred foot boulevard is like a gold-bearing stream."

Within 30 years this gold-bearing stream would be stripped of its glitter and give way to the freeway. Now a congested I-5 is in its third decade and looking for the relief of rapid transit. Much of the old Everett Interurban right-of-way is still intact, a grassy strip for power poles and little parks. It seems to be waiting for the Interurban.

Courtesy of Lawton Gowey

70 Riding the Third Rail to Tacoma

Four fortunate commuters recline at the observation end of one of the Seattle and Tacoma Interurban's plush parlor cars. Two prop themselves upon the ornamental brass railing, another (on the right) exhales a satisfactory puff of cigar smoke, and the fourth looks back into the mahogany interior of the car itself. Inside are 58 pillowy seats where the needs of the line's more affluent riders are attended to by a porter.

Although these parlor cars were colored the same dark green as the rest of the Puget Sound Electric Railway's rolling stock, they were obviously something special, and it cost an extra quarter over the normal 60-cent fare to Tacoma to indulge in their swank comforts. This consumption was made all the more conspicuous by the observation deck, whose pleasures were preserved in the winter behind an enclosure of curved glass.

Using its corporate initials, the PSER advertised a ride resplendent with "Pleasure, Safety, Economy, and Reliability." Electrically-propelled, the trip was free of cinders and smoke, and the "smooth tracks" aided an already "quiet ride." The employees were "obliging," the rates low, and the baggage checked free. Most importantly, the time was fast—on the express, a 75-minute trip which included on the straight stretches the literal thrill of "going like sixty."

When the Interurban began its service in 1902 the automobile was still a sporting novelty for the well-to-do. The popular way of getting to and from Tacoma was via the Mosquito Fleet steamers that buzzed about Puget Sound. The second choice was on the railroad whose "view was terrific . . . the Northern Pacific." Following a similar route down the White (now Green) River valley, the Interurban's scenic path was equally pleasing.

Aiming either into or out of the mountain that Tacoma passengers called "Tacoma" and the Seattle riders, "Rainier," the route passed through hop fields, dairy farms, truck gardens, coal fields, orchards, forests, one tunnel and an Indian reservation. The local, which took 100 minutes to cover the line's 32.3 miles, stopped at places most of whose names are no longer more than a memory of a conductor's urgent shout— spots like Burts, Floraville, Mortimer, Christopher, and Henry. Other stops like Georgetown, Allentown, Renton, Kent, and Auburn are still recited.

Within the city limits the Interurban ran over municipal rails and attached its trolley poles to electric lines overhead. But once out of town and on its own tracks, the trolley would hook up instead with the mysterious "third rail," or contact rail, that ran parallel to the other two that supported the car. This third rail was "alive" electrically.

For the school children along the Interurban's line, this required a special education in the "Four R's"—"Reading, Riting, Rithmatic, and the Third Rail." The lesson for the last was a simple one, "Do not touch it!" Chickens, however, were sometimes encouraged to peck at the grain which was strategically sprinkled along its side. Interurban electrocution was a neat way of preparing a fowl for plucking.

The year 1919 was the most profitable year for the Interurban with more than 3 million passengers. Sometimes a line of six cars were filled with soldiers

Courtesy of Lawton Gowey

Top Before it was paved the Pacific Highway to Tacoma was a mess you might miss in favor of the clean comfort of the Interurban. *Above* The third rail is detectable in this Green River Valley scene. On this straightaway the cars could literally "go like 60!"

returning to Ft. Lewis from weekend romances in Seattle. Within nine years the PSER's haul was cut to less than a third. The completion of highway 99 in 1927 and the proliferation of Model A's meant the imminent demise of the more romantic but regular service both along the third rail and aboard the Mosquito Fleet.

At 11:30 on the Sunday evening of December 30, 1928, the last Interurban cars pulled out from Tacoma and Seattle. The Tacoma bound car left from the intersection of Occidental Ave. and Yesler Way, for 26 years the location of the Interurban depot and the site of both the "now" and "then."

Courtesy of Washington State Historical Society

71 Kent's Carnation

In 1899 the 43-year-old Elbridge A. Stuart left his modest grocery concern behind in Los Angeles and ventured north looking for some business excitement. With the help of a money man named Yerxa and a Swiss evaporator named Meyerberg, he found it in Kent.

From its start as a platted town in the mid-1880s when the railroad first came through here, Kent was not a sleepy town but an ambitious suburb. In the 1880s its big crop was hops, and so it took its name from the County Kent in southeast England where hop harvesting is almost as old as the Canterbury Cathedral, Kent's legendary landmark.

Within a year of his arrival in King County's Kent, Stuart's condensed milk cannery was its principal landmark, and the center of the White (now Green) River's cooperation between cow and man. By 1900 the hop industry had petered out, ruined by bugs and blight, and the local dairy farmers were ready for the entrepreneurial milkman E. A. Stuart.

Stuart converted a relatively new but vacant hotel into his cream-condensing plant. The pleasing two-story brick hotel was built eight years earlier on a rumor that Kent was to be the site of the county's new race track. When it wasn't, pioneer Ezra Meeker used the patronless hotel as a warehouse for his hops until Stuart checked in with his cows and cans.

This 1902 view of the converted

hotel was shot by the photographer Asahel Curtis with his back against the Northern Pacific tracks. He's looking northwest across the intersection of Meeker St., in the foreground, and First Ave. So the signage Stuart has plastered along the long east wall (only) of his plant was for the consumption of the riders and readers on the many coaches and diners that then passed through and paused here at Kent.

This photograph is so well wrought that it is probably a set piece from a free-lance assignment from Stuart to Curtis. On the left, two teams are pulling up Meeker St. with their baggage of milk cans. The bright late morning sky is par-tially darkened with that most conven-tional symbol of that progressive indus-trial age—great billowing black clouds of wealth-producing pollutants. The employee's bicycles are in order and so

Part of the old Carnation plant's rear wall is incorporated into this single story commercial building.

Ezra Meeker,
Kent Pioneer

is the photo's finest effect, the single cow munching on the short grasses that border the rutted street.

According to Kent's official histo-rian Rae Reitan (whose parents both worked in Carnation's Kent plant which they called "the Pen"), Stuart got his name for his milk from a cigar—the Car-nation Cigar. Perhaps since the stogies didn't smell like the flowers, they were soon forgotten in the ashtray, but the sweet milk lived on. Carnation was an inspired and euphonious choice, since it could be alliterated not only with com-pany and cream but with condensed, cows, and, of course, contented as well.

Stuart soon dropped the too scentless and imperious name "Pacific Coast" and rode the back of his Con-tented Carnation Cows to a world enter-

prise with annual sales of 3 billion in 1984, the year Nestle's bought the com-pany. By 1924 the company was already the world's largest producer of evaporated milk.

But by then, after labor troubles in Kent, Stuart had long since moved his evaporators to the town of Tolt on the Snoqualmie River which gratefully re-sponded by renaming itself Carnation. There, on its scientific farms, the com-pany raised a herd of almost bionic Hol-steins that regularly broke world records for milk production. In 1924 its best cow, Segis Pietertje Prospect, produced, all on her own, more than 37,000 pounds of milk and exactly 1,448.6 pounds of butter.

Such a cow was not left to graze at intersections.

Kent and its Varied Resources

The White River Valley is the home of thousands of prosperous farmers---Kent, Washing-ton, is one of its thriving cities

72 South School

It would require either a helicopter or a crane to photograph this "now" from the same spot as the "then." The historical photographer, Asahel Curtis, shot his view from the north end of Beacon Hill. He looked across to grounds that have, since this early-century scene, been radically regraded.

Curtis' most striking subject was South School, the brick edifice on the photo's left. (His wife had been a student there.) First opened to south end kids in 1889, the school barely reached its own maturity when it was closed by the Jackson St. Regrade. In 1909, both the school and its grounds were razed. The

Bailey Gatzert School, we see in the "now," was built on this site in 1921.

A second and much deeper 1909 regrade gouged out most of the ground between Curtis' position and the school's. The Dearborn St. cut went 112 ft. deep, undermining much more than the foundations of the homes in the foreground of Curtis' scene.

The Twelfth Ave. Bridge was completed across the cut in 1912. It was the same steel bridge as that on the right of the contemporary photo, except that it was then topped by a second bridge or timber trestle. The wood addition was necessary because the north end of Beacon Hill was still at its original grade.

In 1923 the hill's north face was washed away. With it, the high-powered jets of water eroded the spot on which Asahel Curtis had set his tripod. The hill was lowered to the level of the steel bridge, and the timbers were removed.

At a 1935 school reunion, South School was remembered as having "the most democratic students Seattle has ever had." The school had probably the greatest ethnic mix in town. It was also remembered as a school of hard knocks, "the toughest school in town," and one of dogs.

The *Seattle Times* story on the reunion quoted Miss Florence Adams, one of South School's retired teachers. She recollected, "I told my class one day that dogs were alright and could come to class so long as the students behaved as well as the dogs."

Courtesy of Seattle Public Library

Above South School students and member of the so-called "Twelfth Street Gang", ca 1900.

Below A classroom scene at South School, about 1901.

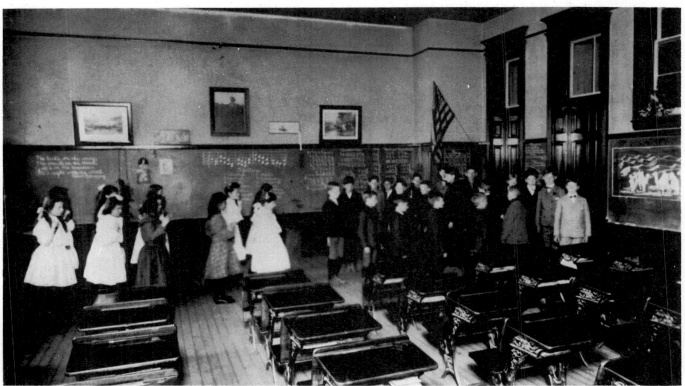

Courtesy of Seattle Public Library

Courtesy of Michael Maslan

73   The Backside of Beacon Hill

It was with uncommon pleasure that I first spied this historical scene— "uncommon" because discovering a good photograph of the backside of any of Seattle's hills is a rare event. View photographers have conventionally never shown much interest in a hill's behind. But this is the north end of Beacon Hill from its rear.

This rare view looks across Rainier Valley to a ridge that is, so to speak, recovered for us in the "time-machine" of this photograph. Here the earth that was removed with the Dearborn cut has been put back on the horizon.

Dearborn is the name of the street in the right foreground of both scenes. But only in the "now" does it continue on west and pass 61 ft. below the bottom of the Twelfth Ave. S. bridge. The top of that bridge is almost in line with the horizon of the lost ridge. From the photo's perspective, where there were

once layers of glacier-compacted clay and gravel, there is now the Kingdome roof as seen through the steel ribbing of that bridge over Dearborn St.

Ralph W. Dearborn was, no doubt, doubly pleased to have this particular street named after him. Dearborn's real estate firm dealt exclusively in tidelands. Not only did his namesake street run into them, but the earth from its excavation helped reclaim 77 acres of the old beach along Beacon Hill. These were the tideland acres that Dearborn then helped sell to the railroads who desperately needed them.

Ralph Dearborn

The original print of this scene appears in a bound album with a title sticker that reads, "Sluicing Work of the Lewis Construction Company presented to R. H. Thomson." Except for this photo, the album's scenes are of the employees of William Lewis and his partner Charles Wiley aiming high-powered water hoses at Seattle's hills. They were probably presented to R. H. Thomson as evidence of their regrading skills along Jackson St. and in support of their bid to do the Dearborn cut as well.

Indeed, this scene, as it appears in the album, has been marked with a black outline indicating the future Dearborn cut. For this printing, I have retouched it away.

Lewis and Wiley got the job, and on September 24, 1909 they began spouting 6 million gallons of water a day at this ridge, channeling the mud onto the

Top Looking east on Dearborn from near 8th Ave. *Below that,* looking the opposite direction across the tracks on Rainier Ave. *Bottom* Some of Beacon Hill that was surrendered to the Dearborn Cut was used to lift Dearborn St. on both sides of its intersection with Rainier Blvd.

tideflats below and piling it up there for Ralph Dearborn to sell. By the time the Twelfth Ave. S. bridge opened in the fall of 1912, they had turned to mud 1,250,000 cubic yards of hardpan, at 20 cents each, and opened a cut 108 ft. deep. Now one no longer needed to go up and down into Rainier Valley but could simply "cut" through to it.

The largest casualty of the Dearborn cut was not old South School (atop the ridge on the right). That red brick landmark was destroyed earlier with the Jackson St. Regrade. This time is was the long shed and tall tower of the Hill Brick Company (right of center). The extended Dearborn St. cut through its kilns and toppled its tower, but since it is an easy thing for a brick business to rebuild, the company survived.

74 Semple's South Canal

*Courtesy of University of Washington
Historical Photography Collection*

Here's one of Seattle's historical believe-it-or-nots. When you ascend Beacon Hill from the Spokane St. interchange off I-5, you are steaming up South Canal.

In 1895, an ex-governor of Washington, Eugene Semple, proposed taking on three herculean tasks at once: the straightening of the Duwamish River into waterways, the cutting of a canal through Beacon Hill from Elliott Bay to Lake Washington, and the reclaiming of 1,500 acres of tidelands with the dredgings from the river and the droppings from the hill.

In July of that year, this ambitious work began with the dredging of the Duwamish River's east waterway. Amid the ceremonial band music, speech making, and inaugural hoopla, the popular Semple promised the crowd that "in about five years" his company would invite them all back "to witness the opening of the locks that will admit a great warship into Lake Washington."

Yet, five years later, the only way to approach Beacon Hill by water was still in a row boat at high tide. By then Semple had reclaimed only 175 tideland acres. His detractors attacked this "specious and mischievous undertaking" to cut through the "quicksands and sliding clays" of Beacon Hill. Instead, they promoted a North Canal, the one that was eventually completed via Salmon Bay and Lake Union.

But Semple would not give up. In the fall of 1901, he attacked Beacon Hill with 4-inch thick jets of water that reached 300 ft. into the air. On November 29 of that year, the *Post Intelligencer* reported that when this hydraulic force was "turned onto the side of the hill, mud, sand, and gravel crumble away like ashes before a cyclone."

This historical photograph accompanied that article which also reported that this "halftone was taken for the *P.I.* by a staff artist who visited the scene of operations in company with Eugene Semple." The photograph's caption read, "End of waterway flume."

You can see that flume running out of the bottom of the historical picture and into the high tide which twice a day covered Elliott Bay's mudflats. The plan, of course, was to direct more mud

Courtesy of Seattle Public Library

The Rainier Brewery just north of Semple's canal.

through this flume and to cover the tidelands below with the hill above. And, for awhile, it worked. Then the soft hill refused to be sculpted for ships and capriciously began to cave in.

Eugene Semple was forced to abandon his South Canal. Today, it has been reclaimed by a greenbelt and the more modest incision of highway engineers. Their work was made easier thanks to Eugene Semple's first cut into his South Canal.

Courtesy of University of Washington Historical Photography Collection

The effect of Semple's attempts to cut into the soft side of Beacon Hill.

Courtesy of Tomio Moriguchi

75 The Flower of Italy

In 1924 or 25, Giacomo and Maria Traverso opened their Fiore d'Italia at 414 Fifth Ave. S., between Jackson and King St. S. These Genoese cooks had the knack for fixing delicious traditional dishes, and soon their cafe was favored for serving the best Italian cooking in the city. Naturally, many of their regulars came from the Italian community, most of whom, the Traversos included, lived in or near Rainier Valley.

The aromas that wafted within this flower of Italy were also for many years the favorite lunchtime relief of the city's garbage collectors, many of whom were, like the Traversos and Christopher Columbus, Genoese. Favorite dishes included: a codfish concoction called Baccala, a generously seasoned cornmeal mush named Polenta, and a meat-and-potatoes mix called Stufato. And every Wednesday Maria Traverso would prepare the week's noodles for the pasta of the day.

The Fiore d' Italia was Traverso's third and most successful attempt at Ital-

ian cooking. In 1917 and 18 the city directories list him at the Pentema Restaurant at 116 2nd Ave. S. But in 1919, with the Pentema closed, Giacomo was recorded by the *Polk Directory* canvassers not as a cook but as a wartime shipbuilder. (Thus, Traverso, may have taken part in the 1919 general strike which started in the shipyards.)

However, as the Traverso's daughter, Jenny Cella, recalls, her father could not be kept out of the kitchen. Soon he was cooking at another skid road cafe, the Columbus Cabaret at 167 Washington St. South.

The mid-20s opening of the Fiore d'Italia at 414 5th Ave. was not the Traverso's last move. By 1928 they shifted their cafe a few doors north to 404 5th Ave. S.—a storefront below the St. Paul Hotel. Still, the Fiore d' Italia was the fixture on a block which saw many alterations.

Appearing in this scene to either side of the cafe are the N. P. Restaurant and the Midget Lunch. Neither can be found in any city directory. The Dreamland Cabaret was a short-lived dive in the St. Paul's basement. It should not be confused with the notorious Dreamland Hotel, a cribhouse for prostitution which was located but a block-and-a-half away at 6th Ave. and King St. (See accompanying photo.)

Fifth Ave., south of Jackson St., could be described as the Mediterranean western border of the International District. There were other Italian establishments on the street including a grocery at the corner of Jackson. Here Fifth Ave. is half a street, for it is bordered on the west by the big pit of the railroad yards and grand stations. And to the east is the East, the international community which is still largely Asian.

This scene was photographed by one of the Traverso's Asian neighbors, Yoshiro Okawa, whose Aiko Photographic Studio was located at 6th Ave. and Jackson St. For years Okawa's fine commercial photography "at reasonable prices" was a neighborhood given—until 1942 when the Okawa family, and all Japanese persons in the district were shipped off to internment.

Since they could take with them only what they could carry, Yoshiro Okawa's years of work were destroyed, including the original negative for this record of the Traverso's cafe. Luckily the print survived. And so did Okawa to open another studio in Chicago after the war. Later he retired to Seattle where he died in 1976 at the age of 85.

Courtesy of Tomio Moriguchi

Above Yoshiro Okawa's Aiko studios above the drugstore at 6th and Jackson. And *above that* the "now" of United Savings. *Top* The notorious cribhouse hotel, the Dreamland at 6th and King Street.

76 Parade of All Nations

William the Duke of Proclamations pronounced six of them for Seattle's first summer festival, the 1911 Golden Potlatch. The first was: "Forget dull care and remember that this is the time for INNOCENT AMUSEMENT."

Recently, two albums stuffed with photographs of these "innocent amusements" have surfaced from the underground of lost or forgotten images. This view of the Afro-American float in the Potlatch's Parade of All Nations is one of them.

On July 21, 1911, the *Post Intelligencer*'s review of this spectacle was headlined, "PARADE OF ALL NATIONS IS SEEN BY GREAT CROWDS...Cooler Day Brings Out Throng For Racial And Industrial Pageant." The article below the headline listed the "races."

Courtesy of Michael Maslan

"After the Japanese Lantern Float, the Cle Elum band led the Italian section. Prominent Italian citizens and their families rode in gaily-decorated automobiles. Then followed the Chinese in automobiles and after them an Afro-American float, which won much applause. The Indians followed…"

The Golden Potlatch was a local creation hybridized from Seattle's enduring fixation with the 1897 Alaska Gold Rush (hence, the "97 Seattle" pennants on the float), and the white man's fascination with the Indian's ritual of gift-giving called the potlatch. In this spirit, another fair spokesperson, a Reverend Major, counselled all citizens to give the gift of "good cheer because it tears down the walls built between us." The clergyman advised that the Parade of All Nations would show how "Every citizen of Seattle is interested in every other citizen…We are a big family."

Wisely, Seattle's Black community arranged their float with girls—the human symbols with the best chance of escaping the grown-up anxieties of racial prejudice. Of course, the reality that awaited them at the end of the parade was the double discrimination held for both black and female. They could return to the love of their own families, but the "big family" would return to making it very hard for them to become anything other than housemaids, nursemaids, cooks, charwomen, or mothers.

Esther Mumford, in her excellent history, *Seattle's Black Victorians*, notes that "Most of the women never realized their importance…Regardless of their marital status, they were at the bottom of society, often poor and ignorant, but it was from that position that women served to undergird the black community by maintaining its basic unit, the family."

Racial discrimination in Seattle was more pernicious in 1911 than it is today. But it's here, and there is still "bad cheer" to dispel if we are at last to respond to William the Duke's sixth and final proclamation: "Apply the Golden Rule to the Golden Potlatch and you will do wrong to no man." Or woman.

Courtesy of Old Seattle Paperworks, Pike Place Market

Left The Italian float in the Parade of All Nations.

Courtesy of Seattle Engineering Dept.

77 Broadening of Broadway

Broadway was once not so broad. North of Harrison St., it was a tree-lined residential street of normal width and modest pretensions. Then, in 1931, it was both spread apart and straightened.

Our older photograph looks north from high above the street's intersection with Harrison. It was shot from the top of a clumsy contraption called a linked-belt bucket ditcher, which was then steadily scooping a sewer trench down Broadway's center—and into our scene. As the sewer went in, the stranded line of power poles near the street's center came down. They mark the original east line of the slimmer Broadway.

The one-story business buildings in this first block north to Republican St. are, with a few exceptions, the same as those still standing. In 1931 they were nearly new. Those on the right side were constructed purposely back from the curb, waiting for the street to spread.

And here on August 24, 1931, Broadway is obliging.

The long building on the left, or west side of the street, is the Broadway Market. Many still remember and miss it. For 30 years, the market served as a block-long collection of independently-owned small shops including a creamery, florist, two delis, fish market, drugstore, beauty salon, two meat markets, health food store, two fruit stands, candy shop, two bakeries, a ten-cent store, and a favorite neighborhood hang-out, Norm's cafe. In 1958, Norm and most of the others moved out, and Safeway and Marketime moved in. Eventually, the windows were stuccoed over, and all the shopping inside was lit with florescents.

It is a subtle and almost always missed fact that while the city's engineers were widening Broadway in 1931, they were also straightening it to conform to the line of Broadway Ave., south of Harrison. You can prove this to yourself if you include this block in your next walking tour of Capitol Hill. A close sighting north up the block's west side from Harrison St. will reveal that the sidewalk shrinks. The Broadway Market, now in the summer of 1986 undergoing its second major remodeling, was built in line with the old Broadway.

In 1904 Fred and Kitty White moved their family into one of the only two houses on the east side of this block.

Bill Burden

Since the primary "now" photo, *left*, was shot in 1984, the windowless wall of Marketime has once again been opened into an arcade.

209

Next door lived Ella Million and her son Ten. (Mother Million emphasized that her son's name was not Tennyson but Ten because "that's what he is to me, Ten Million!") The Whites brought with them from Iowa two Jersey cows, Cloe and Daisy. Thus, the Whites ran what was probably the first "business" on this Broadway block by sending their five-year-old daughter, Frances, to sell Jersey cream to their neighbors.

While on delivery Frances had to watch out for bicycles and electric trolleys. In 1904 the bicycling craze was at its height, and Broadway was a popular and relatively flat route for exercising these brakeless two-wheelers. The trolleys had been running here since the early 1890s when they first cut through the forest on their way to City Park (now Volunteer) and Lakeview Cemetery.

In 1907 Frances moved with her family to the University District. (She now lives in Horizon House.) Ella Million stayed on Broadway until 1930 when her house was razed to make room for a shoe repair store. By that time Ella's son Ten had indeed amounted to something. Ten Million had become a local athletic hero, one of the first Seattle boys to make it into the major leagues as a St. Louis Cardinal. (Unhap-pily, a knee injury from a slide into second base got him quickly out of the majors.)

The tower in the upper right-hand corner of the historical photograph is attached to the Pilgrim Congregational Church. Dedicated in 1906, it was the pioneer church in the neighborhood. In 1931 the congregation lost a part of its front lawn to the Broadway widening, and 18 years later lost the top of its tower to the 1949 earthquake. (This truncated tower is just visible in the upper right-hand corner.

Broadway has gone through many other changes since 1931, but none so physical as its 1931 spreading and straightening. The Million family continued to grow too. Ten had a daughter and named her Decillion Million.

The Silvian Apartments at Harrison St and 10th Ave. E. have lost some of their cornice and bay windows since   ca 1911. On the right of both the "now-&-then" a part of Pilgram Congregational Church is evident.

A TYPICAL RESIDENCE STREET. SEATTLE — Cascade Mountains from Volunteer Park.

78 Millionaire Row & Seattle's Wireless Man

In 1909 Seattle invited the world to its Alaska Yukon and Pacific Exposition, Guglielmo Marconi received the Nobel Prize in physics, and Seattle resident George H. Parker put the finishing touches on his Capitol Hill mansion. The three events are connected.

Visitors to the A.Y.P.'s Manufacturing Building had demonstrated before them the mysteries of Marconi's magnificent invention that would send dots and dashes through the ether with no strings

attached: wireless telegraphy. A.Y.P. visitors were also encouraged to tour the city, and one well-promoted trip was up the 107 steps that climbed the Volunteer Park water tower. From here one could look through 360 degrees of the best available view of the city and its scenic surroundings.

From the water tower one could also look directly down at the new home of Seattle's "wireless man," George H. Parker. The address was 1409 E. Prospect St., and in 1909 the neoclassical mansion rose up on Capitol Hill's clear-cut horizon like a Roman temple, with the water tower to its side. The Parker home was the most imperial touch to this "Millionaires' Row"—14th Ave. E. It was for a time THE neighborhood for the "new rich"; however, George H. Parker's wealth came so fast it was a little too new.

As the United Wireless Company's West Coast fiscal agent, George Parker gave daily thanks to Marconi's genius and to his customers. Only two years earlier in 1907, Parker as a man with but moderate means had moved his family

here from Denver. Now, after selling a few thousand shares of United stock, he was moving into a home with 5 roofed porches, 16 rooms, plus 12 bedrooms, 5 bathrooms, 7 fireplaces, all hardwood floors, muraled walls, adjoining coach house, and his and her automobiles. Parker's $150,000 dollar home was supported by Corinthian columns but his business was a house of cards. In 1909 he would not have long to live or work in either.

Paid for with the Money of a Promoter's Victims

The house that George H. Parker built on fashionable Prospect Street, Seattle, Washington, after he became fiscal agent for the Pacific Coast of the United Wireless Company. Six years ago Parker was poor. The house in the picture was built on land worth $100,000; it cost $75,000, and its furnishing cost another $75,000. Parker was arrested by the Post-Office authorities, and along with C. C. Wilson, president of United Wireless, and others, sent to jail. He is now in the Federal prison at Atlanta. Parker was credited with disposing of nearly half of the $7,000,000 of Wireless stock which was peddled throughout the country

Part of a Seattle Times Cartoon reviewing the city's big news events of 1910.

The banner headline for the June 16, 1910 *Seattle Times* reads: "THE GREAT WIRELESS FRAUD," and the subhead continues: "An Expose of a Giant Swindle and Its Operations in This State. Stock Sold at Forty Dollars Not Worth More Than Two Dollars a Share."

The day before, United Wireless president and Parker's chum, Christopher Columbus Wilson had been arrested in New York City and accused of fraudulent misuse of the mails. It was revealed that Wilson and Parker had been using Marconi's name in vain, for among their company claims was that United Wireless controlled Marconi's companies. It did not.

What they did have was plenty of watery stock but few earthly assets. The ordinary company routine was to enter a town, and, with much supporting promotion, install a $200 wireless station. Then company agents would sell thousands of dollars worth of company stock to that town's citizens. These included "shop girls, teachers, small merchants, retired farmers, policemen, and confiding widows"—most of them easy marks for the show-biz side of high finance.

There were 16 such land stations installed in Washington state. Tacoma's prestigious landmark, the Tacoma Hotel, invited the company to put its station in the hotel's tower. In Walla Walla the city council donated part of a city park for placing the company's station. Typically, the actual broadcasting business didn't even pay for the stations' operating costs. Rather, they were parts of the stock jobbing scheme that built Parker's mansion and an estimated fortune of three million dollars in three years.

Twelve days after the *Times* first headlined the "WIRELESS FRAUD" story, it announced that Parker had also been arrested for mail fraud. Surprisingly, this news was not front page. That, for a week to come, was reserved for features surrounding the upcoming Fourth of July fight between the "Great White Hope, John Jeffries" and black spoiler, Jack Johnson.

Although Millionaires' Row had been touched by a scandal, it was still the city's model neighborhood and was part of every city tour. The primary view printed here is from a tour book, and like most others it was photographed from the top of the 76-foot high observatory. In this instance, the tour book was not promoting class envy but the "city beautiful." Its view south down 14th Ave. S. is captioned, "A typical residence street, Seattle—Cascade Mountains from Volunteer Park." However, here those mountains have been retouched and transplanted to just above Beacon Hill.

Now three-quarters of a century later, the water tower and the mansions are nestled in a new growth of trees nearly as high as the water tower itself. The view down from the observatory is also screened by a double grating of ornamental wrought-iron and thick wire mesh.

From here, the still standing Parker mansion is somewhat lost behind bars, although Parker himself has long since been released from his two year incarceration, which ended on McNeil Island, and has subsequently joined Marconi in the hereafter where everything is wireless. And down to earth, many of the mansions on "Millionaires' Row" have been converted to apartments for "shop girls, teachers, small merchants...and confiding widows."

This 1890 view looking east from Denny Hill shows on the horizon the part of Capitol Hill that but 15 years later would be filling up with homes for the well-to-do.

Millionaire's Row looking north towards the Volunteer Park standpipe under construction. *Below* For a time four mirror reflected spotlights used to revolve along the ring of windows (here reflected in the mirrors) atop the water tower

Courtesy of Seattle Engineering Dept.

79 Republican Hill Climb

Included on the local list of lost places should be the Republican Hill Climb. This elegant stairway was designed to reach higher than the hill. Its grand qualities were meant to be enjoyed for their own sake. And for half-a-century they were.

The climb's design involved three half-block sections. Each was comprised of two single stairways and one double, or branching staircase that circumvented a curving wall.

This view looks east from Eastlake Ave. N. The two men in the scene have apparently chosen to take the northern side of the hill climb's first set of

Genevieve McCoy

branching stairs. They might then have continued on another half block to Melrose Ave., which is just beyond the second curving wall. The very top of the steps is a half block beyond that, and, on the horizon, a third wall that marks it can be seen, barely, just above the second wall. (This top one-third of the Republican Hill Climb is still intact and in use.)

The Republican Hill Climb was approved "as built" by the Board of Public Works on February 25, 1910. This photograph was probably taken soon after that. The landscaping here is still nascent.

Fifty years later, the *Times* published a different photo. It reveals that in its last days this Republican Hill Climb

was pleasantly crowded by tall trees and bushes. The Times caption stated simply, "This stairway will be torn out when the freeway grading begins."

Of course, that "dream road" not only ended the steps from Eastlake but also sacrificed a very invigorating connection between two neighborhoods— Cascade below and Capitol Hill above. But, as City Engineer R. W. Finke explained in 1952, soon after this freeway route was proposed, "Freeway traffic moves at relatively high speed without interference from cross-movements...Pedestrians, who are a constant hazard to city driving, are entirely removed."

We also know that much else was removed besides the pedestrians. Our photograph show us, at least, some of that.

Courtesy of Seattle Engineering Dept.

Top Looking north across the temporary Denny Way overpass during the Freeway's construction. *Above* The construction scene near the Lakeview Blvd. overpass.

The original print for this scene claims that it was photographed from James St. and Broadway Ave. Although captions for historical photographs should be read skeptically, the evidence within this photo (and "behind" it, as well) makes its caption seem right.

If it is right, then what is behind the photographer is Broadway Ave. Up until the turn of the century, Broadway was the eastern limit of "improved" Seattle, the high-class First Hill neighborhood. And what is in front of the photographer is the relatively unimproved plateau that gently descends from First Hill and then rises to Second Hill.

Broadway and James is also a good guess, because for 70 years it was the site of a Seattle landmark, the Union Trunk Line's brick power house and terminal station. Perhaps the photographer was shooting from one of its rear windows. Beginning in 1891 the James St. cable cars completed their climb up First Hill here at the Broadway station, where passengers transferred either to or from the company's electric trolleys that ran up and down Broadway and east to Lake Washington.

Although the photo does not show any of the Trunk Line's service we can see the throughway of another, the Madison Street Cable Railway. Beginning in 1890, the Madison St. cars encouraged and carried settlement all the way to Lake Washington. The part shown here runs from about 12th Ave. on the left, to the street's Second Hill summit at 17th Ave., 422 feet above Elliott Bay, and at the top center of the photograph.

Actually, this ridge that runs across the top of our photograph was as often called Renton Hill as Second Hill. Its namesake was a lumber baron named Captain William Renton. The captain and his hill were remembered by pioneer Sophie Frye Bass in her little book, When Seattle Was a Village.

She wrote: "When Captain Renton acquired the hill it was thickly timbered. When it was logged it presented the sickening sight of all logged off lands—stumps, raw and splintered; saplings, stripped and bent; earth, scarred and torn."

Our photograph which dates from the mid-1890s shows some of that.

Courtesy of Lawton Gowey

Bottom to top A brief pictorial history of the Union Trunk Line's James St. Powerhouse—beginning service on the *bottom* and out of it at the *top.* In the *middle* we see the powerhouse in its heyday. Here passengers switched from-or-to the James St. Cable cars from-or-to electric trolleys that ran north to Volunteer Park, south to Beacon Hill and east to Madrona.

81   Peter Kirk's Kirkland

In the late 1880s a relatively well-off Englishman named Peter Kirk brought his family to Seattle with the ambitious plan to repeat here in duplicate what he left behind on the picturesque coast of the Lake District—a steel mill.

Kirk was industrious, and his English hometown had the least playful name in the entire British Empire. Workington sits beside Moss Bay in the Solway Firth of the Irish Sea, and when Kirk, with the encouragement of *Post-Intelligencer* publisher Leigh Hunt, moved his industry across Lake Washington, he named the bay that fronted his imagined mill, Moss Bay. The projected town, of course, became Kirkland.

Kirk chose the region and his eastside site because Seattle boomers, Thomas Burke and Daniel Gilman, were building a railroad to iron deposits in the Cascades. With their combined dreams of a Workington, or Pittsburgh-of-the-West, attracting thousands of ore-filled gondolas, the already rich Gilman, Burke, and Kirk encouraged one another while understanding that they were still not rich enough. So while looking for

more money in the East, they also, for the sake of both the dream and its appearance, kept building the railroad and the steel mill. But they did have their differences.

Kirk wanted to build his smelters beside Lake Washington, but the capital-poor railroaders refused to run a spur off of their mainline-to-the-mountains all the way into what would become downtown Kirkland. So Kirk had to build his plant up on Rose Hill beside the southeast shore of the pond-sized Forbes Lake (now Lake Kirkland). This change in plans was a disappointment, especially to the speculating horde of lesser Kirklanders who were building a boom town beside the bigger lake. Arline Andre, in her now unfortunately out-of-print history of Kirkland with the punning title Our Foundering Fathers, estimates that in 1890, the year construction began on the mill, there were 5,000 people in Kirkland manufacturing what they believed would be a grand industrial future out of the forest.

However, as far as I can discover, not one of them is in this view of Kirk's mill. Perhaps, this shot was taken in 1893—after the great economic crash of that year. If so, the photographer was somewhat morbidly recording the mortal folly of an industrial ghost town.

The personally protected Burkes and Kirks were not impoverished by this great crash of an industrial dream, but many of the workers and little speculators who sunk their savings into a boom town were.

Fortunately, it seems to me, the Kirkland Iron Works were a failure. Thereby, Kirkland and the rest of us were both saved from future pollution and allowed to develop along more diverse— and playful—lines than those of the English example, Workington.

Even Burke and Gilman's railroad, the Seattle Lake Shore and Eastern, was ultimately given to play, not pay. Two of Seattle's biggest historical boomers are remembered now for their namesake bike trail which runs on the grade of their old railroad, and which, incidentally, never made it to the ore in the mountains.

The lake steamer *Kirkland* rests beside the Leschi Park dock.

Courtesy of Lawton Gowey

82   Issaquah: the Return of the Depot

There's a force in Issaquah working hard to make complete what is now (in 1986) the rough similarity between this "now" and "then." The ultimate goal of this energy is to renovate the old town depot in time for its and the state's centennial celebration in 1889. And it also hopes to bring back the train.

The Northern Pacific R.R. decommissioned this depot in 1958, but many years before that it was the town's life line to the world, and, in fact, a world itself for a platform society of train waiters and train watchers.

The original 1888 coming of the Seattle Lake Shore and Eastern R.R. to Squak (Issaquah's first name) really made the town because, at last, it liberated its coal—coal which had been waiting for a quarter century since the first settlement. In 1862 when a government surveyor named Andrews stumbled upon the Squak Mountain deposits, he soon proved its hot burning quality, but, no doubt, felt the pang of how terribly remote he and his treasure were from the coal hungry hearths of San Francisco.

So it took the service of Seattle railroad promoters, Thomas Burke and Daniel Gilman, using the Squak coal to attract eastern capital, to get the coal (and the name as well) out of Squak. Here the sign across the depot's front gable reads "Gilman," and would until 1899 when "Issaquah," "the more mellifluous rendering of the native guttural "Squak," was substituted for Gilman.

This view of the Gilman-Issaquah depot is reprinted from one of the most delightful histories ever written about a King County community, the late

Above The familiar roofline of the Gilman depot rises above the S.L.S.& E. passenger train. This scene was photographed soon after the depot was completed.

Edwards R. Fish's *The Past and Present in Issaquah, Washington.* Writing in 1964, Fish noted that "in early 1963 the Northern Pacific superintendent of buildings and bridges called for demolition bids. A year later, however, the old building still stands awaiting its fate." Then Fish both added a premonition and planted a seed. He wrote, "Some of us rather wish a way could be found to refit it for an historical museum, since its 19th-century style, ample size, and location in the center of town are all ideal for this purpose."

Enter Greg Spranger and a second premonition. On a visit to Issaquah in 1979, the air conditioner salesman from Anaheim, California, took a stroll with his camera through the center of town. He used it once, for a shot of the old depot which was then a storehouse for tiles. Within the year, Spranger moved to Issaquah and soon became an energetic member of the Issaquah Historical Society and the forceful agent of Fish's vision—or a variation of it—to renovate the depot into a museum of itself.

The list of volunteers that meet each weekend to help Spranger with the renovation includes senior citizens, disabled workers, rail fans, and a hard-working, weight-lifting carpenter Spranger refers to as "King Kong." Actually, the carpenter did not volunteer his skills, rather he was assigned to this public service by a local judge for retribution on traffic tickets. (It occurs to me that this sentence can also be viewed as a kind of poetic justice for the depot and the railroad which were, after all, ultimately eclipsed by the highway and the service station.)

Greg Spranger stands on the left of our "now" scene beside the object of his devotion. His and the historical society's plans also step off the platform and onto the rails. They hope to bring back the train and run a sightseers' excursion service to Woodinville, again, in time for the 1989 state centennial.

At least one structure, the pioneer facade on the right, has survived the 60-odd years that seperate this "now" from "then" on Issaquah's Front St. looking north from Sunset Way.

Bill Burden

Left The old and recently rediscovered and restored Gilman Town Hall.

Courtesy of Issaquah Historical Society

83 James Ditty's Dream of Bellevue

In 1928 King County was searching for a more direct route from Bellevue to Kirkland, so Seattle engraver James Ditty bought up 38 acres bordering what Bellevue historian, Lucile McDonald called the "cow trail known as Peach Street." Ditty renamed it Lincoln Ave. and gave the county its desired right-of-way, and the county responded by paving the old trail. Numerically, the road is 104th Ave. N.E., but it's now called Bellevue Way.

Ultimately, Ditty's dream was not to get to Kirkland quickly but to eclipse it. When James Ditty looked up his Lincoln Ave., he imagined a sprawling commercial center. Perhaps to record the "before" of his dream, he ordered this historical panorama (spliced together from two shots) which looks north across the already paved Main St. (Bellevue's first commercial strip), and up the still rough Peach-Lincoln-Bellevue Way. (Here: the highway sign, left-of-center, still directs the driver west for the old circuitous Lake Washington Blvd. 7-mile route to Kirkland.)

This photo appears in Lucile McDonald's *BELLEVUE: Its First 100 Years*, as does Ditty's grand 1928 birds-eye plan for Bellevue. It's an ambitious arrangement of commerce and amusement featuring: greenbelt-separated factory, home, and market sites; plenty of airports (five including the two envisioned for Mercer island); golf courses, landmark observation towers, and a 64-block-square business district.

Ditty's dream was primarily a bright prognostication of Bellevue Square. But in 1928 Bellevue would still have to wait a few years for a bridge to be built (but not the one Ditty envisioned from Seward Park through Mercer Island), and European fascism to be defeated.

The floating bridge was opened on July 4, 1940 and thereby Bellevue became the principal crossroad between Seattle and Snoqualmie Pass, (and, also, according to a promoter's hyperbole, between Europe and the Far East.)

In 1946 another Bellevue dreamer, Miller Freeman constructed his Bellevue Theater on the conviction that a community was built as much about recreation as industry. Frederick and Nelsons followed in 1947, and, where there were once Ditty's acres of strawberries, poul-try, apples, and stumps, there was, at last, the beginning of his blocks of Bellevue Square.

Miller Freeman came to Bellevue the same year as James Ditty, building his mansion on Groat Point across Meydenbauer Bay in 1928. In sharing Ditty's vision, Freeman added his own convictions which included an almost worshipful respect for convenience. In her Bellevue history, Lucile McDonald credits Freeman with originating what might be considered the archetypal Bellevue slogan, "Parking invites people to come and do business."

Now Bellevue is expanding beyond its parking lots and franchised conveniences into an Eastside city with a glass-curtain skyline. Lucile McDonald, who has written nearly as much regional history as the rest of us combined, was for years a regular in the pages of the old *Times* Sunday Pictorial. She has lived on the Eastside since 1945, and likes it. But the historian in her does reserve one lament when she recognizes that in its explosive growth her home town has obliterated practically every trace of its historical beginnings.

Courtesy of Marymoor Museum

Bill Burden

Looking south through the Midlake Valley then-&-now from Bellevue's NE 8th St.

Now-&-then looking north in line with 116th Ave NE from Northup Way across the site of the old Northup Depot, named after Benson Northup who taught at Seattle's Denny School. The tracks were part of the Lake Washington Belt Line, the Northern Pacific's connection between the Black River Junction (see story *37 Where Bright Waters Meet*) and the S.L.S.& E. tracks at Woodinville.

The original Bellevue school at the site of the present police station.

INFORMATION IN BRIEF

Total Project Length	33,655.76 feet
Total Project Cost	°$7,675,688.45

* *This total does not include costs of right-of-way, engineering and supervision.*

BASIC FINANCING

United States P.W.A. Grant	$3,934,875.00
Toll Bridge Revenue Bonds	5,900,000.00

WORK PROGRAM

Construction Work Commenced	Dec. 29, 1938
Date Opened to Traffic	July 2, 1940

FLOATING STRUCTURE

Number of Standard Floating Sections	10
Number of Special Floating Sections	15
Length of Standard Floating Section	350 feet
Width of Standard Floating Section	60 feet
Depth of Standard Floating Section	14½ feet
Weight of Standard Floating Section	4,558 tons
Height of Roadway Above Water	7½ feet
Height of Rail Above Water	10½ feet
Width of Roadway—4 Traffic Lanes	45 feet
Sidewalks (2)	4 feet
Thickness, Bottom and Outside Walls	8 inches
Thickness, Cell Walls	6 inches
Size of Cell	14x14x14 feet
Number of Cells, Standard Section	96
Number of Water-tight Compartments, Standard Section	12
Length of Floating Draw Span	378 feet
Channel Opening	202 feet
Diameter Anchor Cables	2¾ inches
Weight—Type "A" Standard Anchor	65 tons
Total Number of Anchors	64
Length of Floating Bridge	6,561 feet
Depth of Flotation	7 feet
Maximum Depth of Lake	210 feet

FEATURE FACTS

[1] Largest Floating Structure ever built by man. Weight—approximately 100,000 tons.
[2] First reinforced concrete floating roadway bridge ever built.
[3] Reinforcing steel equal to 700 miles of 1½-inch square bars used in pontoon construction.
[4] Cost of floating structure and bridge approaches approximately $500.00 per lineal foot.
[5] Weight of Floating Structure 13 tons per lineal foot.
[6] Total number of cells in floating structure—1900.
[7] An average expenditure of $16,000.00 was made every day over the 18-month construction period, Jan. 1, 1939, to June 30, 1940.
[8] During the entire construction not a single fatality to workmen.
[9] Short wave radio was used in locating the anchors.

BASIC TOLL:

Passenger Car and driver, 25 cents.

For further information address:

WASHINGTON TOLL BRIDGE AUTHORITY
Transportation Building
OLYMPIA, WASHINGTON

Lake Washington FLOATING BRIDGE SEATTLE, WASHINGTON

BIGGEST THING AFLOAT IN THE WORLD—

An early promotional piece for the then new Mercer Island tollbridge.

84　From Willowmoor to Marymoor

In 1904 James Clise, a 49-year-old banker from Seattle, purchased 78 acres beside the Sammamish Slough near Redmond. Clise's first intent was to have his own English moor or game preserve, and so he built a hunting lodge and named it Willowmoor after the trees that lined the slough.

But this was just the beginning, for the sportsman Clise soon developed into a industrious gentleman farmer. Within three years he increased his holdings to 350 acres and soon his hunting lodge spread into a 28-room Tudor style mansion.

Clise imported a heard of Ayrshire cattle from Scotland, and bred them with a success that brought awards, international study, and a sweet protein-rich milk whose reputation reached even the nation's dairyland, the Midwest. When Henry Ford built a hospital for his employees in Michigan, he insisted that only milk from Clise's Ayrshires or their descendants be served.

By 1917, the year his doctors pre-scribed a move to California for his fail-ing health (now patients are as often sent this way), Willowmoor was a model milk industry with 40 employees. The plant was made up of 28 buildings includ-ing: sheds, barns, bunkhouses, a black-smith's shop, a boathouse, a narrow-gauged train, several homes for workers with families, including Clise's English gardener, and a library for his employ-ees.

The Clise family's constructions included: an elaborate tree house for their

two boys and a girl; a windmill some-times outfitted for parties with huge revolving canvas sails; and a gallery, windowless except for the skylights which shed a proper light on the family's art collection, which, like their gardener, cows, and windmill, were brought back from Europe.

For Mrs. Clise there were also two large pergolas for the exhibition of her roses and four greenhouses for the cultiva-tion of her exotic orchids. (The orchids were eventually given to the Volunteer Park Conservatory,where some of them still survive.)

The Clise mansion was so wide that our older view of it was printed onto two panels—thus the intruding centerfold. That the most evident difference between our "now" and "then" is in the landscape, not the home, is due to the good sense of King County voters, who in 1963 saved Willowmoor from commercial development and made a park—Marymoor Park.

The name change from Willow to Mary occurred in the early 1940s when one of the later owners of the Clise properties, Walter Nettleton, memorial-ized his daughter Mary, who had died years earlier in a bike accident in Seattle.

As a part of Marymoor Park, ten rooms in the north wing of the Clise mansion were dedicated to use as a histor-ical museum. Then in 1973, the Marymoor mansion itself was placed on the National Register of Historic Places. Now in its 19th year, the Marymoor Museum features: rooms that are theme decorated and appointed, outreach pro-grams, a growing archive of Eastside his-torical photos, and, opening this past September 7, 1986, the special exhibit "Homestead to High Tech—The Eco-nomic Development of the Eastside."

The Marymoor Museum is open 4 days a week. Call 885-3684 for exact times.

Bill Burden

above & below Two now-&-then comparisons of the Redmond business intersection of Leary Way and Cleveland Street.

85 Mercer Island — C.C. Calkin's East Seattle

Genevieve McCoy

By the late 1880s, Seattle had grown big and rich enough to attract its first suburban dreamers. C. C. Calkins was one of them. In 1887 this 34-year-old, Wisconsin-trained lawyer with a temperament too speculative for mere law, landed in Seattle with $300 in his pocket. Within two weeks, he was $19,000 in debt but 21,000 acres richer. Some of that land was attractive enough that he soon resold it, cleared his debt, and was left standing cleanly on $170,000 worth of property.

While his peer promoters were building band stands and dance pavilions on the remote shores of Lake Washington at Leschi and Madison parks and connecting them via cable cars to the masses huddled beside Elliott Bay, Calkins went one step further to Mercer Island. There he platted and soon produced East

Seattle—a playland for Seattle's well-to-do, replete with fountains, turkish baths, a boathouse filled with 100 boats and 28 dressing rooms, and this grand hotel.

The details of Calkin's East Seattle are told well in Judy Gellatly's book, *Mercer Island, the First 100 Years*. She writes that "Calkin's hotel was a source of pride and a great marvel to the Mercer Islanders" who themselves were still "laboring mightily just to exist." The hotel's main floor featured an immense ballroom and a large dining room. From a big hall, the grand staircase led conspicuously to the upper floors which were divided into large parlors and 24 guest rooms. The hotel's appointments were equally lavish with tiled floors, designer wallpapers, and fancy hand-colored plaster work featuring cupids, baby angels, and bouquets.

In 1891 President Benjamin Harrison embarked from Leschi Park on C. C. Calkin's namesake steamer for a visit to East Seattle. It was a moment of brief but soaring success for both Calkins and the islanders. But it was also, alas, penultimate to the visit of that great destroyer, the International Crash of 1893, which dropped the speculator Calkins to his knees, and left the hotel standing empty for years.

In 1902 a search for an appropriate use was somewhat grimly answered by a Major Cicero Newell who used it as a home for delinquent boys. When the major's East Seattle neighbors objected to his habit of chaining his boys to the fence, the Major, rather than foresake his punitive principles, abandoned the hotel.

Thereafter, the grand hotel was used sometimes as a retreat for the treatment of alcoholics, and at other times as a boarding house. But it was as a summer hotel that it came to its spectacular conclusion in 1908.

That July, soon after its last proprietor Dr. Leiser smilingly opened it to his fair weather guests, he made the mistake of scolding one of his house boys who responded by burning down his hotel.

The dry timbers of the tall Gothic landmark made a fire so spectacular that, as a preventative, the nearest houses, some 200 feet away, were covered with wet blankets.

Eva Helbsy, who stands at the center of our now scene, moved to East Seattle in 1910 when the ashes of Calkin's grand hotel had barely cooled, and the story of its spectacular destruction was still fresh. She led us to the site of that Mercer Island retreat for Seattle's wealth.

C.C.Calkin's grand plan for his East Seattle.

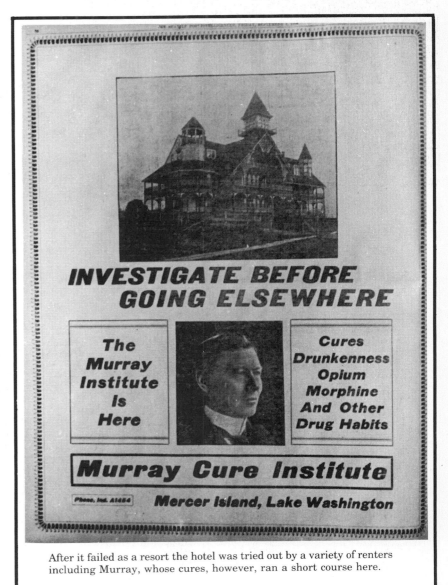

After it failed as a resort the hotel was tried out by a variety of renters including Murray, whose cures, however, ran a short course here.

Courtesy of Old Seattle Paperworks, Pike Place Market

86 Arcadian Art

Northwest author Murray Morgan, left with some of the "Wits of Wilson Point."

Recently a friend who buys and sells old photographs in the Pike Place Market showed me a new discovery: two tableaus photographed somewhere on the shores of Puget Sound in which women, mostly, have arranged themselves in artful poses. Both of these unusual scenes are equally exquisite, so I have included them both.

Agreeing that it looks like Puget Sound, where on its shores are these women aesthetically conspiring with the artist-photographer? His name was John Wagness, and for a few years around 1890 he had a studio in Tacoma before he moved north to Stanwood. So is this the south Sound? Yes, for happily on the back of one of these art cards an antique hand has lightly penciled in a florid style the name "Arcadia."

Arcadia! How that name resonates with the classics—Shakespeare, Milton, Sidney. It was in the fields and forests of that legendary Greek landscape where young singing shepherds—and English poets—fell in love, not with their sheep, but with perfect shepherdesses with names like Philosclea and Pamela. And there they were enraptured with Arcadian nature itself, "the fair rocks, goodly rivers, sweet woods, and delights of solitariness." Arcadia was that wonderful dreamland where art and nature played together.

And so these artful posers are doing it properly in Arcadia, Mason County, Washington state, Greece-U.S.A.

If you look on your Mason County map, you'll find there still is an Arcadia on the south Sound. The 1901 *Washington State Directory* characterizes it as "a post office on Puget Sound...10 Miles E. of Shelton, the Mason County seat, and about 12 miles N. of Olympia." But long before there was a Shelton, there was an Arcadia. As Deegan's old *History of Mason County* simply states: "The first settlement at Mason County started in the vicinity of the first logging operation. These were at Kamilichi and Arcadia, first called Arkada."

Sitting at the opening to the county's two southern waterways, Totten and Hammersley Inlet, Point Arcadia was an important intersection in the tangle of the south Sound's saltwater highways. Deegan's history claims that for "30 years, up until Sheltonville became Shelton in 1888, the people of the sur-

rounding country got their supplies from Olympia or often from Arkada." At one time this hamlet had a post office, general store, restaurant, saloon and, as the 1872 *Puget Sound Business Directory* predicted, "a very promising future."

What happened? Well, settlements on points exposed to the commerce on the water, but dead ends on the land, are not likely to flourish when the highways are paved, not waved. Today Arcadia is still on the map but the businesses are long gone. The point is now a green suburb of Shelton with homes so restful and secluded that there one might be moved to write some verse about the "sweet woods and fair rocks."

And that, thankfully, is what makes Arcadia, Mason County and a lot of

Puget Sound much more like the poets' legendary land than is that land-locked and rock-infested plain on the Greek Peloponnesian peninsula which is the real Arcadia.

I confess, I have never been to any Arcadia, except in poetry. But I have been very close—only 4 ½ miles as the crow flies east of Arcadia—at the idyllic beach scene on Harstene Island's Wilson Point. To get there, this crow would have to cross two channels and the Squaxin Indians' island reservation before it could alight on the rustic Mason County cabin of Murray and Rosa Morgan. It was there that I photographed this contemporary beach view with its collection of characters who themselves have had some success in joining art and nature.

Index

The Book's INDEX is listed in reference to story numbers not pages. (The reason for this departure from conventional index form is somewhat involved, and is explained in the book's introduction.)

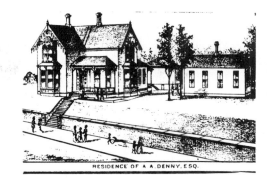

RESIDENCE OF A. A. DENNY, ESQ.

Boyd 713 FIRST AVE. SEATTLE.

There are so many histories to write. Now that this *Volume II* is completed I can begin again on *THE AVE*, a hundred-year history of a street—*University Way*. Any readers of Volume II are encouraged to remember their own AVE pasts, if they have them, and confess them to me. I am in the book. Another history to write is KRAB's...the now-silent-listener -sponsored-radio-station-looking-for-a-new-frequency. While preparing *Volume II* I listen to all my cherished last-week-of-KRAB tapes, and realized how deaf I am with its silence. Here is a wonderful record of the old KRAB at its old home on Roosevelt Way. Some of the characters in this scene should be familiar to you.

Seattle 1902

If you should like to receive a signed copy of this book in the mail, send $25.00 for the hardcover, or $12.95 for the paperback to *TARTU PUBLICA-TIONS* P.O.Box 85208, Seattle, WA 98145

FINIS